CAROLS
FROM
KING'S

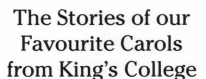

The Stories of our
Favourite Carols
from King's College

ALEXANDRA COGHLAN

1 3 5 7 9 10 8 6 4 2

BBC Books, an imprint of Ebury Publishing
20 Vauxhall Bridge Road,
London SW1V 2SA

BBC Books is part of the Penguin Random House group of companies
whose addresses can be found at global.penguinrandomhouse.com

Penguin
Random House
UK

This book is published to accompany the radio series entitled
A Festival of Nine Lessons and Carols from King's College Cambridge,
first broadcast on Radio 4 in 1928.

Series Producer: Philip Billson

First published by BBC Books in 2016

This edition is produced exclusively for Heffers

www.penguin.co.uk

A CIP catalogue record for this book is available from the British Library

ISBN 9781785940941

Commissioning Editor: Carey Smith
Project Editor: Grace Paul
Illustrations: Mai Osawa
Cover design: Two Associates
Production: Helen Everson

Printed and bound in Great Britain by Clays Ltd, St Ives PLC

Heffers and King's have had a close association for many years, from the days when the recording department used to sell records and tapes rather than CDs. Perhaps one of the most notable of these early recordings was the ground-breaking 1964 45rpm of Allegri's Miserere, which – together with the BBC broadcast of the Nine Lessons – brought the music of King's to a worldwide audience.

At Heffers we look forward with interest to each new project from the Choir. Recently we have seen the launch of King's own label, with releases which illustrate the dynamism and variety of music coming out of the Chapel: from Evensong to the close harmony of the King's Men, the organ recitals of Stephen Cleobury and, of course, the Festival of Nine Lessons and Carols.

The publication of this book is a wonderful opportunity to celebrate not only the music of King's, but also one hundred and forty years of music and book selling at Heffers. We're delighted to mark the occasion with a new CD of Christmas music to tie in with the book, produced in association with Warner Music. The album is a survey of carols from the past half-century, from the era of Sir David Willcocks up to the present day, culminating in those under Stephen Cleobury. These wonderful recordings of the carols, together with the fascinating stories behind them, are perfect companions in a traditional Christmas from King's.

For John Nourse

CONTENTS

PREFACE

by Stephen Cleobury

My first awareness of the Festival of Nine Lessons and Carols arose when, as a chorister at Worcester Cathedral in the early 1960s, I heard the late Sir David Willcocks being interviewed on the radio about this service. I never heard it in its entirety then as the cathedral choir had its own duties on Christmas Eve. A number of the points David made about choir training have remained in my mind and been immensely useful to me ever since. But all those years ago I could never have imagined that one day I would assume the responsibility of being the guardian of the great tradition of the King's service. Still less can I have thought that I would have the privilege of being involved with it for over 30 years.

I remember Christmas Eve 1982, my first at King's, vividly. I entered the chapel at about 2.30 in the afternoon to prepare myself for the start at three o'clock. Those who had patiently queued from early in the morning were by then seated and listening to the organ music which the organ scholars play before the service begins. I was struck by the wonderfully calm atmosphere and the sense of waiting and anticipation among those present. The idea of 'waiting' is one of the themes of Advent, the season in the Church's year which precedes Christmas and properly finishes on Christmas Eve. Waiting and anticipation are not often available to us in our busy modern lives, nor even in church, to the regret of many of us.

Perhaps the defining moment of the service comes at the start, when one of the choristers starts to sing 'Once in Royal David's City'. Millions listening around the world to BBC World Service and in the UK on Radio 4 wait for this moment. This is, for many of those who write to me, the 'beginning' of Christmas. I often feel that the familiarity of this hymn and its association with a young child singing the solo prevents me from appreciating properly the poetry of Mrs Cecil Frances Alexander. Here is a simple and moving statement about the journey of life: God, in the person of Jesus Christ, 'came down to earth from heaven' to be among us, to feel and share the sadness and the gladness in our lives, and to guide us, in the end, to 'the place where he is gone'. This is the traditional Christian understanding and the service speaks directly and powerfully to those who associate themselves with this. I think that its breadth of appeal, however, is wider. Those who have been nurtured in this tradition but who have in one way or another departed from it tell me that they can respond at this special time of year to the retelling of the Christmas story which follows in all manner of deeply fulfilling ways. I know, also from my correspondence, that many who have no faith or who come from other religious traditions can be deeply moved by the combination of words and music, which, at the simplest level, tell the human story of the birth of a young child.

As well as preparing the choir for the Christmas Eve service, a process which takes place following the Procession for Advent some four weeks before, I need to have chosen the repertoire well in advance. In this, it is the combination of words and music which is of utmost importance. I aim to find a judicious mixture of old and new, the text of each carol chosen needs to reflect some aspect of the preceding reading and the whole has to form a satisfying musical sequence. Only the second of these criteria can be judged objectively. It is part of the pleasure of my work to receive comments on the first and third. While I naturally enjoy the appreciative comments more than the critical, the latter are, however, extremely important in making me think carefully the following year.

In each of the years I have been at King's, except in my first when there was not time to set things up, I have commissioned a new carol (sometimes the chosen composer has also commissioned new words). I feel strongly that such a great tradition needs to have 'new blood'. Initially, some were not so appreciative of the new pieces, though among the earlier ones both John Rutter's 'What Sweeter Music' and Judith Weir's 'Illuminare, Jerusalem' have achieved considerable popularity. As time went on, however, I found myself increasingly being asked 'Who is writing the new carol this year?' I have been very fortunate in that no composer I have approached has refused the commission. A number of those who have written are not primarily known for writing sacred choral works, but it is important to me to show that Church music does not inhabit a backwater unconnected with the mainstream of musical expression in the opera house and the concert hall.

A contemporary survey of carols from King's would not be complete without reference to the television programme of that name which, although it began in 1954 on an irregular basis, has been an annual broadcast since the early 1990s. This retains most of the elements of the traditional Radio 4 radio broadcast, most particularly in that it begins with 'Once in Royal', but with the help of successive deans and chaplains, and an excellent working relationship with the producers, it intersperses poetry and prose within a sequence of familiar biblical readings. (More recently still, there has been a television broadcast *Easter from King's*, which presents the events of Holy Week and Easter in a similar format.) This has been widely welcomed. The broadening of the scope of the readings has enabled a particular focus to be placed each year on a different aspect of the Christmas story. This in turn has given me new opportunities for repertoire selection.

I count myself extremely fortunate to have been able to play a part in the maintenance and development of this wonderful tradition.

INTRODUCTION

Once in royal David's city,
Stood a lowly cattle shed,
Where a mother laid her Baby,
In a manger for His bed

(Mrs C.F. Alexander, 1818–95)

It's 3pm on Christmas Eve. The last of the light catches the greens, golds and deep reds of the stained-glass windows of Cambridge's King's College Chapel, scattering their colours like precious gems across the stone floor below. Caught in this half-light, animated by the flickering candle flames, the fan-vaulted ceiling seems liquid, dripping down the walls in magnificent stone icicles.

The organ plays, softly, but above the music rises a hum of voices. The chapel is full, packed from the top of the chancel, watched over by Rubens's *Adoration of the Magi*, to the West End. Everyone waits for the arrival of the choir. Only the microphones slung low from the roof bear witness to the millions of others who also listen and wait. They might be in Yorkshire making mince pies or in New York wrapping Christmas presents, but with the radio switched on, they too are here in King's Chapel.

Suddenly the organ stops, and the only sound is the slight rustling of surplices and robes – heard, or perhaps only imagined. The choir, bright in red and white, are in place, grouped close together under the Tudor carvings of the West End. The director of music stands in front of them, waiting. At last he raises his arms, points to one chorister. The boy steps forwards and starts to sing: 'Once in royal David's city, / Stood a lowly cattle shed, . . . '

Christmas has begun.

What's most striking about this scene – the chapel, the choristers, the candles – is its timelessness. We could be in any decade of almost any century, celebrating a ritual that seems as old as the chapel itself – maybe even older. At least, that's the impression we get.

What's really astonishing about the service of Nine Lessons and Carols is just how recent a phenomenon it actually is. A service that seems so ancient, so embedded in the history and identity of this chapel, this college community, was in fact only celebrated here for the first time in 1918. And it wasn't a revival of a historic tradition, a return to an immemorial model. Nine Lessons and Carols was the creation of just two men: Edward Benson, Bishop of Truro, and Eric Milner-White, the young dean of King's.

In less than a hundred years, Nine Lessons and Carols has become a touchstone of Christmas, celebrated not only in churches and cathedrals across the UK but right around the world. But what is it about this service, this particular combination of words, music, light and architecture that has so captured the public imagination?

For many it's the moment of pause it offers – stillness at a time of year filled with noise and chaos, a meditation by any other name. For others it's the sudden shock of beauty. Whether you're hearing the service for the first time or the fiftieth, the effect is always the same; emotions aren't so much stirred as seized, shaken out of you by a ritual that assaults all of your senses. It's also a rare service that reaches beyond a Christian community, speaking potently to those of different faiths or even no faith at all with the unusual, unmediated directness of its readings and music.

More potent even than the service's imagined history is its real genesis. Fresh from the horror of the First World War, faced with a disillusioned, broken community and a college and a nation that could no longer find consolation in the formal liturgy of the Anglican Church, Eric Milner-White brought Bishop Benson's Nine Lessons and Carols to King's, reshaping it into the service we know today. The service is simple – just 'nine carols and nine tiny lessons' – and it's precisely this simplicity, this directness, that is its strength and power. It's a service that excludes no one and welcomes everyone, from 8-year-old choristers to their 80-year-old grandparents.

But if Nine Lessons and Carols is an invented tradition, then so are the carols that form such a big part of it. Their roots might stretch all the way back to the medieval period, but it wasn't until the nineteenth century that they became the popular, sacred songs we'd recognise today – played or sung in every home, church, school and shopping centre each December.

Thanks to the wide reach of its radio, and later television, broadcasts, King's service of Nine Lessons and Carols has played a huge part in bringing carols back into the mainstream during our own century. Hard though it is to believe now, there was a time when even the best-loved favourites – 'While Shepherds Watched', 'Ding Dong Merrily on High', 'O Little Town of Bethlehem' – were in danger of being forgotten, something for specialists to study rather than people to sing.

This book explores the history both of King's service of Nine Lessons and Carols and the carols that feature in it. Along the way we'll encounter Romans and reindeer, kings and choristers, pagans and Puritans, and discover the stories and secrets behind some much-loved pieces of music.

What was the partridge doing in the pear tree? Was good King Wenceslas really all that good? And how exactly did three ships manage to sail into the landlocked town of Bethlehem? All these questions and more will be answered and the history behind favourite festive traditions including Christmas cards, trees and carol-singing explained.

We'll also take a look behind the scenes at King's itself, hearing from the choristers, composers and the directors of music who have shaped the service of Nine Lessons and Carols, and learning just a little more about Eric Milner-White, the man whose imagination, vision and humanity started it all.

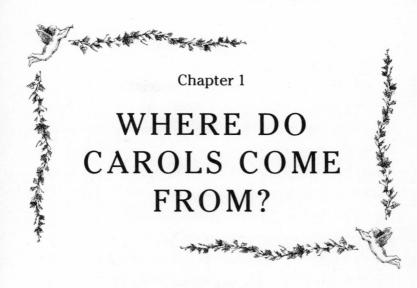

Chapter 1

WHERE DO CAROLS COME FROM?

Here we come a-wassailing
Among the leaves so green;
Here we come a-wand'ring
So fair to be seen.

(Anonymous, seventeenth century)

What's the first image that comes into your head when someone mentions Christmas carols? Small choirboys in red robes and white ruffs? Or perhaps a country church, stained-glass windows brightly illuminated, spilling the sound of congregation and organ out into a cold night? What about Victorian carol-singers, lantern aloft, hark-the-heralding on the village green, or Tudor feasts – all candles, mistletoe and music? School concerts with cardboard donkeys and tea towel-wearing Wise Men? No? Then maybe it's the endless, purgatorial loop of tunes piped through department stores each December?

All of these images are part of the carol's history – important parts – but none of them quite captures where it all began. Not in church, at court or even in the home, but in fields, woods and streets. And it wasn't choirboys, vicars or polite congregations singing these first experimental, exploratory carols, it was peasants – ordinary people singing and dancing in joyful celebration. Because carols haven't always been precious and sacred. In their earliest form they were muddy, rough-spoken and sometimes even rather rude – subversive songs that spoke louder of pagan feasts and festivals than they did of Christian miracles.

To understand what Christmas carols really are (as opposed to what the Victorians have brainwashed us into believing they are) we have to scrub them clean of the layers of paint and gloss that have obscured their original, rough-hewn forms. We have to leave the ordered beauty of King's College Chapel and travel back in time, trace Christmas itself back to its origins – a journey more unexpected, more exotic than anything undertaken by Ebenezer Scrooge and his ghostly guides.

It's a journey that will take us from debauchery in the Roman Empire to folklore and fertility rituals in pre-Christian Scandinavia before we can return safely to England, Cambridge and the Christmas that we all know and love.

THE FIRST CHRISTMAS CAROL

Carols have been around since the moment of Christ's birth and the first one even makes it into the Bible. The angels appear to the shepherds, telling them of the birth of Jesus. Then, according to St Luke's Gospel: 'Suddenly there was with the angel a multitude of the heavenly host praising God, and saying, Glory to God in the highest, and on earth peace, good will toward men.' This angel chorus cuts to the heart of what Christmas carols are all about. These aren't sophisticated anthems, they are simple, joyous songs capable of capturing just a little of that angelic wonder and communicating it to us all in words and music we not only understand but can share in.

What the Romans Did for Us

Picture the scene: it's December, normal work has been cast aside and people exchange work and study for celebration and relaxation. Children, freed from the schoolroom, run and play in streets lit by hundreds of burning torches and candles, while in the town squares food and flagons of wine are laid out on long tables – a feast for all, noble and peasant alike. People drink and eat, dance and sing, and drunkenness is all but obligatory. Friends and families exchange presents, sometimes perfume and clothes, sometimes books and even animals.

It's a set of traditions that sounds very familiar – eating, drinking, singing, giving gifts. But this isn't Christmas. In fact, it's probably all taking place before the birth of Christ. Welcome to Saturnalia – the Roman festival of the god Saturn and a feast far wilder than even the most uproarious family Christmas today.

Roman mythology celebrated Saturn as the ruler of the Golden Age – a mythical time of plentiful harvests and eternal summer, a time before wars and conflicts, hierarchies and labour, when man and nature lived in happy harmony. Once a year, each December, the Romans would attempt to recreate this blissful state for a period of one week, hoping to please the god into delivering them from winter barrenness and restoring warmth and crops.

During this time everything was turned upside down: cross-dressing was popular, with some people going one step further and dressing up as animals, work was exchanged for play and children (normally silent and very much at the margins) took centre stage in the festivities. Most importantly, masters and their slaves swapped places; the masters would wait on their slaves, while the slaves in turn would criticise them freely and even give orders, in a complete reversal of everyday life.

Leading the revelry, and driving it on to ever-greater extremes, was the Saturnalicus Princeps – the king of

DID YOU KNOW?

Saturnalia wasn't all fun and games. Sometimes the Roman festivities took a decidedly dark turn. One particular group of Roman soldiers, based in what is now Austria, celebrated the festival each year in a rather unusual way. Thirty days before Saturnalia they would choose a young, handsome man from among their group to act as Saturn himself. During those 30 days he would indulge in every possible pleasure – however sinful. But when the festival arrived the young man would have to go to the altar of Saturn. There he would cut his own throat – an offering and penance to the god he had impersonated.

Saturnalia. Each household or town would draw lots and whoever won would take command for the duration of festivities, issuing orders (the ruder or more ludicrous the better) which had to be obeyed, taking charge of gambling and stirring up a gleeful chaos without consequence or punishment. Whether you were commanded to strip naked and run through the streets or impersonate a bear, you did it – no questions asked.

But then Christianity arrived. Out went Saturn and his fellow gods, replaced by just a single god – one who didn't smile upon the deviance and debauchery of his predecessors. Roman citizens were, understandably, reluctant to give up their celebrations and abandon their traditions, and so an uneasy alliance was born between pagan and Christian customs.

In the fourth century AD celebrations of Christ's birth – initially commemorated on 6 January – were moved to 25 December, to coincide with Saturnalia. It was a strategic compromise; the people could once more keep their favourite holiday traditions, simply transferring their enthusiasm from Saturn to Christ – from sun to son – a simple substitution that harnessed all the energy of the pagan festival, but channelling and redirecting it to new Christian ends.

Yule

Saturnalia is the mischievous grandfather of one set of Christmas traditions – presents, party games, overindulging – but in order to find others – the Yule log, Father Christmas, bright lights around the home – we now have to don furs and gloves and travel many miles, to the north of Europe. Here, in countries starved of the sun, plunged into almost total darkness for many months each year, the winter solstice was something worth celebrating. Once this shortest day (and longest night) of the year was past, things would only improve. The festival was one of hope, of anticipation of better things to come.

Just as Saturnalia had its candles, so the Scandinavian festival of Yule had its fires and torches. Not only were these symbols of the much-wished-for sun, but also weapons against the forces of darkness – demons, both mythological and rather closer to home. In many ways this feast was a celebration of pragmatism. With days so short, so little light and no farming to be done on the frozen ground, the chances of despondency and depression setting in were high. Add in the need for a little extra food to help people survive the winter and you have the roots of a midwinter festival that sustained Northern Europe for centuries, eventually crossing over to England with the Vikings who ensured that the early Anglo-Saxon Christians celebrated their Christmas with a healthy sprinkling of pagan traditions.

One of these traditions – Father Christmas – has had a particularly long journey from his earliest days to today's familiar figure, with his twinkling smile and long white beard. One of the principal gods of Old Norse mythology, Odin (known to the Anglo-Saxons as Woden) was a particularly important part of a Scandinavian Yule. This magical figure, with his long beard and cloak, would travel through the skies on an eight-legged horse called Sleipnir, leaving gifts in the shoes of any children who had been thoughtful enough to leave food for his horse. Today's Father Christmas might no longer have an eight-legged horse, but he does have eight reindeer instead.

And then there's the Yule log – another pagan custom the Christians retrospectively claimed as their own. A symbol of the sun in the darkest winter months, the log was traditionally large enough to burn from Christmas Eve all the way through to Twelfth Night. Originally a piece of oak, chosen to honour Norse god Thor, when the custom arrived in England it was decreed that ash should be used instead, as ash was said to be the wood used to heat the water to wash the infant Jesus after his birth.

Whatever the wood, however, the tradition remained the same. The log must burn for the full span of the festive season. If it went out for any reason, it was an omen of bad luck for the year ahead. Each year as the log burned down to its final few hours some of the wood would be saved in order to light the following year's fire – a sign of the eternal light of heaven. Ashes from the log were said to have magical properties and were scattered into wells to keep the water pure and around the base of trees to promote a good harvest.

And so Christmas arrived in England – a mongrel festival, incorporating customs and myths not only from Ancient Rome and Scandinavia but also Persia, India, Germany, Greece and Egypt. It's only fitting that a festival such as this, assembled piecemeal from so many different parts, should have a soundtrack of a similar kind – music that has passed through many pairs of hands, each leaving their own distinctive imprints on it.

'THE HOLLY AND THE IVY'

Although this charming carol, based on an English folk tune, probably dates from the seventeenth century, its symbolism is far older. Both the festivals of Saturnalia and Yule placed great emphasis on evergreens. The Romans would exchange boughs of holly and ivy with their friends during the festival, while both the Scandinavians and the Anglo-Saxon pagans would decorate their homes with the evergreens they saw as symbols of eternal life. So try as Christian carol writers might to impose their own symbols on the plants – the red holly berry as Jesus's blood, the white holly flower his shroud – they have to work hard to displace earlier layers of meaning. Some think there's a further secret layer of meaning to the carol. Is the holly, with its phallic prickles, a symbol of the masculine, and the clinging ivy of the feminine? English courtiers were fond of such hidden language and holly-and-ivy carols could have formed the basis of courting games.

What is a Carol?

True Christmas carols are like myths or legends, they've always existed, but they come from nowhere. Nobody wrote the words or sat down with pen and paper to compose the tune, but somehow they just are, part of the pool of collective memory that we all share – touchstones of tradition.

But this isn't a book about 'true' carols. If we stuck closely to the strictest of definitions then neither 'Hark! The Herald Angels Sing' nor 'Away in a Manger', nor even 'O Come All Ye Faithful' would qualify, leaving our festive celebrations rather sad and tuneless. So instead of worrying too much about the technical details, which carols qualify and which don't, I propose a rather simpler criterion.

'A song intended to mingle joy with wonder.' That's a Christmas carol according to nineteenth-century carol collector William Wallace Fyfe and it's a definition that has a lot going for it. For a start we've thrown out any complex musical requirements. A song is anything written to be sung, it can take any form, can be any length or in any style. And then there's the breadth of emotions. Between them, joy and wonder pretty much cover the whole gamut of Christmas music, embracing 'We Wish You a Merry Christmas', 'Joy to the World' and even Slade's

'Merry Xmas Everybody' at one end and everything from 'In the Bleak Midwinter' to 'Have Yourself a Merry Little Christmas' at the other.

WHAT'S THE DIFFERENCE BETWEEN A CAROL AND A HYMN?

Carols appear in hymn books alongside hymns and they deal with the same biblical subjects in the same kind of verse, so how do we tell the difference between the two? The simple answer is that, nowadays, we often don't. Carols and Christmas hymns happily coexist in our carol services and we have no problem with 'The Holly and the Ivy' (carol) jostling elbows with 'Hark! The Herald' (hymn). But if you really want to tell them apart, the easiest way is to ask yourself whether the music makes you want to tap your feet. If the answer is yes, then you can be pretty sure it's a carol. In more absolute terms, hymns tend to grapple more directly with theology, while carols are content to narrate biblical stories or meditate on biblical figures in more poetic terms. If all else fails, listen out for the burden–refrain structure (see page 12) – another good clue that you're listening to a carol.

Admittedly the 'mingling' is more problematic. Not every Christmas song we know and love blends joy and wonder in equal measure. But stop and think about it and it's only the rarest exception that doesn't have at least a touch of each – a glimpse of something delicate, inexpressible somewhere in the background of all that riotous jollity.

It's true to the spirit of carols that we're not completely certain where they, or even the word itself, come from. Some say the word derives from the Greek for dance – *choros*, others from the Old French for dance – *carole*, or the Latin term *choraula* which was a choral song. What's interesting here is how important a role dancing plays – something we know was true of the earliest English carols.

These carols weren't songs at all. They were round dances – dances that would take place in a circle. So central was this idea of the circle to the carol that twelfth-century chronicler Geoffrey of Monmouth described Stonehenge as 'the giants' carol'. The carol dances would often be accompanied by singing and took a very specific form. Each would consist of two parts: a stanza (what we might think of today as the verse) and the burden (a sort of chorus). What's distinctive about a burden, setting it apart from a contemporary chorus, is that it doesn't just feature between each verse; it also starts and closes the carol.

While the stanzas might be accompanied by a few instruments or improvised by a solo voice, the burden would probably have been something that everybody joined in with, either in song or dance – a communal gesture of musical joy, probably set to a catchy tune. Sound familiar? It's here that we see the first glimpses of the carol as we know it today.

It's worth pointing out though that at this stage carols had no particular connection to Christmas, but were danced and sung at any time of year. They crop up frequently in Chaucer's (c1343-1400) writings, the word used simply to mean a dance with song. In his *Romaunt of the Rose*, for example, Chaucer's narrator is invited to join the dance:

> *'Come, and if it lykè you*
> *To dauncen dauncith wih us now.'*
> *And I, withoutè tarrying,*
> *Wente into the karolying*

There were carols for every occasion. You could have a hunting carol, an Ascension carol, an Easter carol or even – as in the case of the 'Agincourt Song', which celebrated the victory of Henry V at the Battle of Agincourt – a political carol.

While the dancing element of carols didn't last long, echoes of these origins can still be clearly heard in a number of carols we sing today. Take 'Ding Dong Merrily on High', for example. Its gloriously catchy melody, with its swinging refrain, was originally exactly what it sounds like – a dance, one known as Branle de l'Officiel (Dance of the Official).

First written down by Frenchman Thoinot Arbeau in the sixteenth century, what was probably originally a folk tune was then transformed into the carol we know by George Ratcliffe Woodward, a nineteenth-century Anglican hymn writer who composed some preposterously archaic words ('Let steeple bells be swungen') to suit this ancient melody. Elsewhere we also see hints of medieval stamping feet and tapping toes in carols such as 'Deck the Halls', the lively French 'Patapan' and the lilting dance of 'In Dulci Jubilo'.

But all this is still a few centuries in the future. What kind of carols would people actually have been singing in medieval England? What would they have sounded like and where would they have been singing them?

One particularly rich seam of carols from the medieval period and beyond has grown out of the curious tradition of wassailing.

'ALS I LAY ON YOOLIS NIGHT'

Cradle songs are one of the most popular forms for medieval carols and one of the loveliest of the genre is surely 'Als I Lay on Yoolis Night'. This anonymous fourteenth-century song is sung by the Virgin to the infant Jesus. It gives us a poignant insight into the relationship between this heavenly child and his very human mother. She wishes he would go to sleep without a lullaby, but the baby demands a song ('The child him thought sche ded him wrong, / And bad his moder sing'). She demurs, explaining that she barely knows him; the first she knew of her child was when the Angel Gabriel appeared to her. It's an unusual conceit, this conversation between mother and child, but one that explores the emotional implications of the Annunciation. The plainsong melody lilts gently, rocking the baby with simple, repetitive rhythms even as the melody roams and wanders like the mother's own thoughts.

Wassailing

Wassailing has a good claim to being one of the very oldest Christmas customs, with roots that stretch all the way back to the fifth century. The word 'wassail' (originally the Anglo-Saxon *waes hael*) simply means 'good health'. It was a greeting shared among acquaintances and the expected response was '*Drinc hael*' ('Drink and be of good health'). Initially that exchange of good wishes was all there was to it, but by the twelfth century the emphasis had moved firmly on to the '*Drinc hael*' and the wassail bowl was born.

In the days leading up to Twelfth Night, the final day of the Christmas festivities, groups of villagers would make their way around the neighbourhood carrying the wassail bowl – a large bowl made of anything from silver to wood, filled with hot cider or ale that was richly spiced with sugar, nutmeg, cinnamon and cloves and topped with pieces of toast. At each house they would sing and present their bowl and it was the householder's duty to drink from it (refusal brought with it a year's bad luck) and then offer the wassailers food and drink in return.

It's a tradition that makes sense of the rather strange words to carols such as 'We Wish You a Merry Christmas', explaining why the singers are demanding 'figgy pudding' so confidently and why it needs to be brought 'out here'. And it's in these wassailers that we see the forefathers of today's carol-singers, travelling from house to house offering their songs in return for food and drink.

The 'Gloucestershire Wassail' is just one of many carols intended to accompany this progress, and its verses give us a vivid description of the wassailing process itself.

Wassail! wassail! all over the town,
Our toast it is white and our ale it is brown;
Our bowl it is made of the white maple tree;
With the wassailing bowl, we'll drink to thee.

Here's to our cow, and to her long tail,
God send our master us never may fail
Of a cup of good beer: I pray you draw near,
And our jolly wassail it's then you shall hear.

But what started as an innocent custom, a way of spreading good cheer and good luck at the turn of the year, sometimes took a slightly darker turn. The wassailers were often groups of young men and with so much alcohol involved the custom could easily turn rowdy or even downright violent. Gangs of wassailers would demand drink and even money from rich landowners, threatening to vandalise their homes if they were not satisfied, rather like an adult version of today's Halloween trick-or-treating.

A more wholesome variant of the tradition, popular in the West Country, was the orchard-visiting wassail. This involved the wassailers, led by their wassail king and queen, gathering in local orchards to drink the health of the trees and wish them a good harvest in the following year. Pieces of toast soaked in the wassail would be placed on the branches and roots of the trees, while pots and pans were banged and clattered in hope of waking the trees up from their winter slumber.

The custom's most famous carol – 'Here We Come A-wassailing' – seems to combine both the orchard and house-visiting versions of the tradition. The verses ('Here we come a-wassailing / Among the leaves so green;') are sung to a marching tune, perfect for putting a spring into steps possibly trudging through snow and certainly in cold conditions, while the refrain ('Love and joy come to you, / And to you your wassail too') is a softer affair – almost a blessing.

The carol we know today isn't an authentic medieval work, but a ragbag of musical shreds and patches. Like so many carols this one has been written and rewritten by many generations, picking up a rhythm here and a melody there along the way. But what we are left with, carefully cleaned up by the Victorians, is a carol that gives us a vivid flavour of a tradition that endured into the twentieth century.

First wassailers gave way to the waits – official bands of musicians who patrolled cities at night and played music to wake citizens on dark winter mornings. These in turn morphed in the mid-nineteenth century from a professional ensemble to an amateur affair, limited to making music at Christmas time, and now we have carol-singers – their natural descendants.

In *Cider With Rosie* (1959), Laurie Lee's evocative memoir of a Gloucestershire childhood between the wars, the author gives us a glimpse of this tradition in transition. Not quite wassail, nor yet contemporary carol-singing, it's nevertheless filled with riotous Christmas cheer and music-making of authentically dubious quality. Each year the young Lee and his friends head up to 'the Big House', singing all their favourite carols. The singing might have been poor, but the welcome was always warm, and as an ancient community tradition it was unimaginable for Christmas to happen any other way.

Mystery Plays

The twentieth century might have been the first to have cinema to spread its catchy Christmas songs, but in many ways it was just imitating a far older tradition. Medieval Britons couldn't head to see Bing Crosby crooning 'White Christmas' each December, but they did have their own festive entertainment – plays. Oddly, given the carol's secular roots, it wasn't the pantomimes or mummers' plays with their colourful cast of characters (including an early incarnation of Father Christmas) that gave us the best of this music, but their sacred cousins – the mystery, or miracle, plays.

As early as the fifth century, enterprising clerics were enhancing their services with living tableaux – visual translations of Bible stories the congregation might otherwise only hear in Latin. These early liturgical dramas gained scope and ambition over several centuries until eventually they combined both spoken dialogue and sung chant. But these were amateur dramatics compared to the elaborate mystery plays that would take place outside the church.

Perhaps it was their secular context that gave these plays the freedom they needed to put drama first, or perhaps it was the professional pride and rivalry of the various guilds of artisans and tradesmen who would take responsibility for different sections of the plays. Whatever the reason, these dramas became hugely popular, drawing large crowds to the streets, churchyards and marketplaces where they were performed.

The Pageant of the Shearmen and Tailors is one of only two plays that survive from the cycle of mystery plays performed annually in Coventry to mark the feast of Corpus Christi. Dating from the fourteenth century, it tells the story of the Nativity from the Annunciation through to the Massacre of the Innocents – a dark and unusual climax to the drama. It's this story that gives us the context for one of the loveliest and most unusual of all Christmas carols – 'The Coventry Carol'.

> *Lully, lulla, Thou little tiny Child,*
> *By, by, lully, lullay.*
>
> *O sisters too, how may we do,*
> *For to preserve this day*
> *This poor youngling for whome we do sing*
> *By, by, lully, lullay.*

Without a little background the carol at first seems both baffling and out of place in Christmas celebrations. Why is it so mournful and slow, more like a funeral dirge than a song of joy? Who is the baby being rocked to the refrain

'Lully, lulla' if it's not the infant Jesus? And who are the 'sisters' who do the rocking?

The carol's story is a sombre one. Herod, hearing that the king of the Jews had been born in Bethlehem, and fearing his newborn rival, commands that all children in the city under the age of two should be killed. In the pageant, the carol comes just before the arrival of Herod's soldiers. Some mothers run and hide with their children, holding them close and hushing their cries with this dark lullaby, while others grab any weapon they can and prepare to defend their babies. But it's no use. The soldiers kill them all.

Unusually bleak and subject specific, the music for 'The Coventry Carol' was probably written especially for the play and not adapted from an existing folk song. The original carol manuscript has the music written out in three-part harmony – sung by three mothers who, confusingly, would have been played by men. This harmonisation, the interaction between the three voices, is absolutely crucial to the particular character of this carol.

A melody is not enough here to capture the tensions and emotional conflicts of this unique situation. Sing the top line on its own and you have a nice enough tune – nothing special. But add in the lower voices and suddenly there's this heartbreaking friction between the simple lullaby melody and the piercing dissonances – musical doubts –

The Coventry Carol

thrown up by the harmonies beneath. It's as though the mothers, doing their best to calm their children, can just about manage to sing a familiar lullaby, but cannot quieten their own fears and uncertainties. These haunt the lullaby and turn comfort and familiarity into something altogether less certain.

And then there's that extraordinary final chord. Just listen to the refrain – it's all in the minor and is persistently sad, mournful. But then, out of nowhere, we end each verse with a major chord, suddenly happy, but why? Is it a final, defiant gesture of hope from the mothers? Or is it the final twist of the knife – the cruel grin of a soldier dispatching his bloody duties? Either way it's extraordinarily potent music, a carol that offers a shocking reminder of the dark subplot of the Nativity.

Music in the Medieval Church

While wassailers were singing their way through the English countryside and the mystery plays were delighting audiences in the towns, what was happening in church during the twelfth and thirteenth centuries? The medieval Church had plenty of music – and good tunes at that.

There were the great office hymns – 'Stabat Mater', 'Pange Lingua', 'Veni Creator Spiritus' and – for Christmas – the lovely 'A Solis Ortus Cardine'. These weren't hymns as we know them today. There was no organ accompaniment (or accompaniment of any kind, for that matter) and these sinuous plainsong melodies would be sung in unison by whole religious communities or congregations. They rarely had anything resembling verses and choruses; they were just a continuous flow of melody, at once simple and unadorned and highly sophisticated.

Beautiful though these plainsong hymns were, they weren't exactly festive, and there soon came a time when clerics and congregations alike were longing for something just a little more catchy – something less academic, possibly even something not entirely in Latin. But although the urge was there, progress was slow. Carols, with their association with dance, were seen by puritanical English society as somehow sinful, their seductive rhythms highly suspicious. How could they possibly welcome such worldly music into their churches?

Slowly but surely, however, things began to change. First came the arrival of 'singing men'. For the first time music in cathedrals and larger churches would be sung not by the clergy themselves (a guarantee of decidedly mixed quality) but by professionals. They not only improved the standard of music dramatically but also changed the kind of music being composed and sung. Suddenly anything was possible and the result was a flourishing of more complex and inventive compositions.

In the thirteenth-century we get sequences such as the charming 'Angelus ad Virginem' – a carol in all but name – sneaking into services as processional music. At last! A melody that sticks in the ears, that people would have found themselves humming on their walk home. Lilting dance rhythms set the story of the Annunciation and Nativity to a tune that skips with barely suppressed joy, begging for some instrumental accompaniment, maybe even some percussion, to help it along. After the austerity of plainchant we've also got some rudimentary harmonies to jazz things up still further, adding the new bold possibility of variation between verses.

The Franciscans Bring Carols into Church

But if it wasn't for the Franciscans, 'Angelus ad Virginem' and its ilk might have been the beginning and the end of festive musical celebrations. This practical order believed in reaching people by any means possible. It was they who first introduced crib scenes into churches – first human, then made of clay or wood – believing that they helped convey the Christmas story more effectively than any sermon.

Seeing the popularity of secular folk carols, the Franciscans took the best and most successful of their melodies and wrote new religious words for them. Carols, like the eye-catching stained-glass windows, were a teaching tool, another way to reach a simple congregation drawn to beauty and melody. Once again, the Christian Church was cleverly insinuating itself into the shell of pagan and folk traditions and claiming the space as its own.

As a device it proved enormously successful and from 1400 onwards we see a sudden flowering of new carols, fuelled both by the skills of the singing men and the canny work of the Franciscans. One example is the exquisite carol 'There is No Rose of Such Virtue'. Following the classic carol burden–stanza structure, it is at once entirely simple and embellished with infinitely skilful delicacy.

The carol combines words in two languages, English and Latin. Slipping freely between the two, it meditates on the Virgin Mary, comparing her beauty and purity to that of a 'spotless rose'.

> There is no rose of such virtue
> As is the rose that bare Jesu;
> *Alleluia.*

There is No Rose of Such Virtue

The lovely imagery of the anonymous verse is echoed in a melody that contents itself with the very simplest of burdens – almost every note follows the one before it in step, with no dramatic leaps, and the rhythm scarcely varies – with a verse that unfolds with the same organic, almost improvisatory grace as the heavenly rose itself. Two vocal lines wind and weave their way among one another like growing stems – an artistic gesture of faith as lovely as any medieval icon.

The Virgin Mary was a popular figure for early carol writers and numerous cradle songs and lullabies from this period survive. The fifteenth-century 'Song of the Nuns of Chester' is an unusual, transitional carol. It combines a plainchant hymn 'Qui creavit caelum' ('He who made the heavens') with a simple lullaby refrain 'Lully, lully, lu' between each line. The effect is magical, at once divine and human, sacred and secular.

A slightly later example is 'Sweet was the Song the Virgin Sang', which pairs a contained, inward sort of stanza with a suddenly expansive burden – differentiating between the earthbound music of the narrator, 'Sweet was the song the Virgin sung, / When she to Bethlem Juda came', and the Virgin herself, who expresses her love for her child in music of fluid beauty and grace, 'Lulla, lulla, lula, lullaby'. The effect is magical.

'In Dulci Jubilo'

But if there's one carol more than any other that captures the spirit of the medieval Christmas it's 'In Dulci Jubilo'.

This piece, originally a German chorale but enthusiastically adopted by the English, combines the dance of the original secular carol with sacred words that themselves embrace both Latin and the vernacular (either German or English, depending on where you are singing it). It's a proper hotchpotch – a joyous mixture of all that's best about Christmas music.

MACARONIC CAROL

Nothing to do either with macaroni or even macaroons (disappointingly), a macaronic carol is simply one that uses two different languages. 'In Dulci Jubilo', for example, combines words in Latin and English, though the text is so well known that you almost don't notice. Generally, though not always, macaronic texts are a clue that the carol has its roots in the medieval period.

In Dulci Jubilo

The story behind the carol's creation is also a good one. It was written by Heinrich Seuse, a Dominican monk, in 1328. Legend (supported and, one suspects, fostered by Seuse's biography) has it that one night the monk was sitting in his cell, when an angel appeared to him, commanding that he cast off his sorrows and join him in a heavenly dance. Seuse took the angel's hand and found himself suddenly dancing and singing a glorious song about the Nativity:

> *In dulci jubilo,*
> Let us our homage show!
> Our heart's joy reclineth
> *In praesepio;*
> And like a bright star shineth
> *Matris in gremio.*
> *Alpha es et O!*

It's a story with echoes of the Nativity itself – of the angels appearing to the shepherds – and captures something of the spontaneous outpouring of joy that all the greatest carols express. It helps that the carol's melody is one of the very best – a light-footed dancing tune that (depending on tempo) either skips or steps in more stately fashion – and musicians from every century have been drawn to it, remaking it in the fashion of their own day.

The version of 'In Dulci Jubilo' most often sung at King's actually dates from the nineteenth century. Composer Robert Lucas Pearsall took this simple carol and transformed it into something much more sophisticated, but without losing any of its beauty. The musical bones of the piece are so strong that Pearsall was able to manipulate them substantially, not only harmonising them in new ways but also embellishing and even reworking them completely for his chosen forces of five solo voices and four choral parts. The effect is radiant and graceful, constantly seizing the ear with a new texture or melody. No wonder it's among the most-performed carols at the annual service of Nine Lessons and Carols.

The medieval carol is, above all, a paradox. At once sacred and secular, pagan and Christian, home-grown and imported, a solemn song and a lively dance, it's the product of an age still under construction. That's its charm. How many genres can embrace everything from rowdy, bawdy songs to sophisticated, sacred music, or claim contributors ranging from peasants to bishops and everyone in between?

If the Victorians take credit for renovating the carol, for wiping off the dust and cobwebs and painting it fresh and new, then the medieval Britons must take credit for building it in the first place. Like their churches, these medieval carols may have been rugged, functional affairs, architecturally solid rather than decoratively ornate, but they have endured the wind and weather of changing tastes and fashions. Christmas in the twenty-first century may look very different to Christmas in the fourteenth, but, thanks to so many medieval musicians, it still sounds remarkably similar.

Chapter 2

A TUDOR CHRISTMAS

The boar's head in hand bring I,
Bedeck'd with bays and rosemary.
I pray you, my masters, be merry
Quot estis in convivio

(Anonymous, fifteenth century)

It's Christmas Day 1540 and as a courtier of Henry VIII, one of Europe's most splendid monarchs, you head to Hampton Court to celebrate. Dressed in your finest furs and silks you ascend the stairs to the Great Hall, the smell of cloves, cinnamon and nutmeg filling the air. Hundreds of beeswax candles light your way and as you approach the chamber itself the sounds of revelry – laughter, music, chatter – spill out into the stairwell. Suddenly the doors are flung wide and you find yourself in the royal presence.

Seated up on a dais at the far end of the room is Henry VIII. The light from the torchbearers glints off the jewels of the ladies and the magnificent display of gold and silver plate that lines the room, drawing the eye from the tapestries that cover the walls and the dark boughs of holly, mistletoe and ivy that frame them.

A bowl of lambswool – hot ale, spiced and rich with sugar – is thrust into your hand. You drink and pass it on, while around you courtiers break into song.

> *Pastime with good company*
> *I love and shall unto I die;*
> *Grudge who list, but none deny,*
> *So God be pleased thus live will I.*

Now the feast begins. Trumpets sound, heralding the arrival of the boar's head on a platter. But this is only the prelude to the real climax – the arrival of the peacock. Skinned and roasted, the bird has then been replaced within its own cured skin, still covered in feathers. Carried in by no fewer than six servants, it is placed upon a bed of edible 'grass' – a glorious centrepiece for all the pies, meats, pastries and sweets that surround it. Drinking and eating continues into the night, while above in the gallery minstrels play.

Suddenly the king commands silence for the masque and everyone gathers round to watch the elaborate spectacle. Masked players enact their drama, helped by the most magnificent props. A gilded chariot draws gasps, but a fully working fountain raises cheers and applause. It's dawn before the last of the carousers have left, reluctant, but comforted by the knowledge that it will happen all over again in just a few weeks' time, for the feast of Twelfth Night.

The Tudors took their Christmas celebrations seriously and – unlike us – their festival lasted not just a single day but the full 12, from 25 December to 6 January. It was a period of release, a chance to throw aside the hardships, privations and strict rules of the rest of the year and let loose. But even the Tudors didn't have the stamina to keep it up for almost two weeks. The high points – days of all-out excess – were Christmas Day, New Year's Day and Epiphany, and between them celebrations were rather more muted.

The rules of the festive season were, in their own way, just as strict as those of the rest of the year. Women were forbidden from spinning, and no work at all was permitted except the care of animals. What was encouraged was a reversal of all typical hierarchies. Schoolboys could lock their masters out of their schools, only allowing them to return once they had conceded to demands for longer playtime and fewer lessons.

In churches, chapels and cathedrals a boy bishop might be appointed. For a single day (often 6 December, the feast of St Nicholas, or Holy Innocents' Day on 28 December)

DID YOU KNOW?

A Tudor Christmas may have been a drawn-out and indulgent affair, but people had to earn it. Advent was a period of fasting, with the Christmas Eve fast being particularly strict – no meats, eggs or even cheese permitted. Even Christmas Day itself wasn't without a more serious side. It was usual for people to attend not just one but three Masses on Christmas Day, the first one beginning well before dawn. So by the time you were munching your goose and mince pies you really had earned them.

this chorister or altar boy would be endowed with all the authority and duties of a bishop. He would preach a sermon, visit the poor, lead processions – everything short of actually taking Mass. The practice was banned in 1541, however. Henry VIII, now the head of the Church, took issue with the ancient custom that he now saw as a direct attack on his own authority.

A similar tradition continued, however, in villages, households and courts, where a lord of misrule (the clear descendant of the king of Saturnalia we met in the last chapter, see page 4) would be appointed for the festive season. Elevated from his usual status, this lord would take charge of all celebrations, encourage riotous games and act as a sort of mock king until Twelfth Night when his powers would disappear and he'd return to his original status. The lord of misrule's revels often got rather out of hand (neither Elizabeth I nor Mary I permitted the custom for this reason) and one courtier reported a year when celebrations included the release of a fox and a cat in Inner Temple Hall. The animals were hunted by a pack of hounds until both were torn to pieces.

Secular Carols

But where did carols fit into all these celebrations? The Tudors were certainly fond of their Christmas carols and singing them was an important part of celebrations, but only rarely in church. Singing them in a religious context at all was still a fairly new innovation and they featured sparingly. Occasionally a carol such as 'Angelus ad Virginem' might be

DID YOU KNOW?

If you live in England there's a very good chance that you are breaking the law every Christmas Day without knowing it. In 1551 Edward VI passed a law stating that all citizens must walk to church on Christmas Day. It has never been repealed...

used as processional music and the more meditative Passion carols of composers such as William Cornysh, John Browne and Richard Davy might also be used as anthems.

But it was outside the church – at court and in the streets, alehouses and people's homes – that carols really flourished. Their words could be sacred or secular, it didn't matter; all were seen as a natural part of the festivities, a way of celebrating the Nativity not only in prayer but also in raucous song.

It's hard to think of a more typical Tudor carol than 'The Boar's Head Carol'. Not only was it one of the very first printed carols – published in the earliest-known English collection of carols, Wynken de Worde's *Christmasse Carolles* – but it captures the spirit of feasting and merry-making that was at the heart of the Tudor Christmas.

> The boar's head in hand bear I,
> Bedeck'd with bays and rosemary.
> And I pray you, my masters, be merry
> *Quot estis in convivio*
>
> *Caput apri defero*
> *Reddens laudes Domino*
>
> The boar's head, as I understand,
> Is the rarest dish in all this land,
> Which thus bedeck'd with a gay garland
> Let us *servire cantico.*

Caput apri defero
Reddens laudes Domino

Our steward hath provided this
In honour of the King of Bliss;
Which on this day to be served is
In Reginensi atrio.

Caput apri defero
Reddens laudes Domino

But what is the significance of the boar's head and why do we celebrate it? The story behind the carol is one of the most colourful of its kind – a proper home-grown folk tale that, while it has its roots at Queen's College, Oxford, also has a long history just up the road from King's at rival college St John's, where the feast has been an important part of the annual college calendar since the seventeenth century.

Legend has it that one Christmas Day a student at Queen's College set out to walk to church through the woods outside the city. Lost in his copy of Aristotle, he paid little attention to the landscape around him until a loud grunt startled him from his book. He saw a wild boar standing in front of him, poised to attack. The quick-thinking student promptly plunged his Aristotle down the beast's throat, incapacitating it, then finished him off with a spear (why he was carrying a spear to church remains unclear). He carried his prize back

The Boar's Head Carol

1. The boar's head in hand bear I, be-
2. The boar's head, as I un - der - stand, is the
3. Our stew - ard hath pro - vi - ded this, in

decked with bays and rose - ma - ry; and I pray you my mas - ters
rar - est dish in all the land, which thus be - decked with a
hon - or of the Queen of bliss, which on this day shall be

be mer - ry, *quot es - tis in con - vi - vi - o.*
gay gar - land, *let us ser - vi - re can - ti - co.*
ser - ved is, *in re - gi - nen - si a - tri - o.*

Ca - put a - pri de - fe - ro, red - dens lau - des Do - mi - no.

to Queen's and that night the whole college feasted on it. To this day, the Boar's Head Feast is still celebrated at Queen's, complete with boar.

Frustratingly, Wynken de Worde's carol book survives only as a fragment. 'The Boar's Head' is the final carol in the book and it alone remains today. The page gives us the words for the carol, not the melody – printing technology simply wasn't capable of reproducing music at this point – but the traditional tune that has since attached itself to the verse is a jolly, shouty sort of affair. Verses are sung unaccompanied by a soloist, interspersed with a rousing four-part chorus. It's not hard to imagine it being performed at Henry VIII's court to accompany the ceremonial arrival of the boar, with everyone joining in the chorus.

'Deck the Halls'

One popular sixteenth-century song that would not have been sung at court, however, was the carol we know today as 'Deck the Halls'. Back then it was a favourite Welsh song and would have been known by its original title 'Nos Galan'. It wasn't until the nineteenth century that it acquired Christmassy words and became part of our own festivities. In its earliest form, 'Deck the Halls' was just a folk song, but one with some rather naughty words. Translated directly, the Welsh text reads something like this:

> *Oh! how soft my fair one's bosom,*
> *fal lal lal lal lal lal lal lal la:*

> *Oh! how sweet the grove in blossom,*
> *fal lal lal lal lal lal lal lal la:*
> *Oh! how blessed are the blisses,*
> *Words of love, and mutual kisses,*
> *fal lal lal lal lal lal lal lal la:*

These words would not have suited the prim Victorians, so when Thomas Oliphant came to write an English text for the melody in the 1860s he started from scratch, co-opting the dancing melody and lively 'fa la la' chorus for an altogether more innocent celebration of Christmas preparations.

Deck the Halls

A Christmas Conundrum

Of all the Christmas carols we sing today, none presents more of a challenge than 'The Twelve Days of Christmas' with its baffling list of lyrics. The words are secular, meaning we get no immediate help from the Bible, so what exactly are we to make of this aviary of birds – the swans, geese, doves, hens and calling birds – and what on earth is a partridge (strictly a ground bird) doing up a pear tree?

The origins of the carol make things a little clearer. Although historians are unsure as to when the carol was first known, they do generally agree that the verse first evolved as a festive memory game, along the lines of Grandmother Went to Market or The Minister's Cat. The list of objects or animals grows with each verse and forfeits are imposed for anyone forgetting one.

But that still leaves us with the problem of the partridge. While the English partridge is a creature of fields and moors, its French cousin is apparently a little more athletic, more likely to find itself up a tree – of any species. And if the partridge really is French then it would be called *une perdrix*. Correctly pronounced 'pere-dree', suddenly this word sounds an awful lot like that pear tree that was causing so many difficulties earlier. Could it, perhaps, just be an elaborate international game of Chinese Whispers that has left us with a partridge stuck forever in a misheard pear tree?

There are more interpretations of this carol than almost any other, but many of the explanations come back to religion. One particularly compelling one places the carol's origin in the sixteenth century. The list of bizarre gifts given by the carol author's 'true love' become a secret code for Catholics – whose religion had to be practised in secret after the Reformation – to share their beliefs. So the 'true love' becomes God himself and the partridge (French or otherwise) Jesus Christ – a gift given to all believers. And so it continues: 'two turtle doves' are the Old and New Testaments, 'three French hens' the Trinity, 'four calling birds' are the Four Gospels, all the way through to 'twelve drummers drumming' – the twelve points of the Apostles' Creed. We'll never know the truth of this strange little rhyme, but if you were a Tudor child, wouldn't you much rather recite this than your catechism?

Sacred Carols

So far we've only looked at secular Tudor carols, but there were also a growing number of a more religious hue, often taking the Nativity or the Virgin Mary as their theme. One of the most intriguing of these is 'I Saw Three Ships', a carol that – like 'The Twelve Days of Christmas' – isn't all it seems. Let's just pause over the words for a moment:

> *I saw three ships come sailing in,*
> *On Christmas Day, on Christmas Day,*
> *I saw three ships come sailing in,*
> *On Christmas Day in the morning.*

And what was in those ships all three?
On Christmas Day, on Christmas Day,
And what was in those ships all three?
On Christmas Day in the morning.

Our Saviour Christ and his lady,
On Christmas Day, on Christmas Day,
Our Saviour Christ and his lady,
On Christmas Day in the morning.

Oh, they sailed into Bethlehem,
On Christmas Day, on Christmas Day,
Oh, they sailed into Bethlehem,
On Christmas Day in the morning.

A couple of issues immediately present themselves. Bethlehem, as any atlas will attest, is an inland city with no nearby river, so anyone 'sailing in' really would be a Christmas miracle. Then there's the question of why just two passengers (Mary and Jesus) required three ships, especially when one of them was still in his mother's womb. And where was Joseph during all of this? The lyrics pose more questions than they answer.

Explanations are legion. Do the three ships perhaps represent the Holy Trinity? Or what about the Three Wise Men? The latter have the most plausible link to the carol. Legend goes that about 300 years after the birth of Christ

I Saw Three Ships

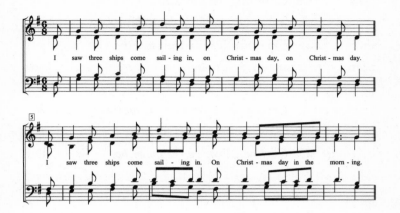

I saw three ships come sail - ing in, on Christ - mas day, on Christ - mas day.

I saw three ships come sail - ing in. On Christ - mas day in the morn - ing.

the bodies of the Magi were transported to Cologne by Empress Helena, mother of Constantine, as holy relics for the new cathedral. The precious cargo travelled in state in three separate ships and their arrival into the city must have been quite a spectacle. Enough to inspire a carol? Quite possibly.

Musically, 'I Saw Three Ships' is a charming carol and its light, dancing melody is a natural fit for the unusual first-person narrative. This isn't a collective story, like 'We Wish You a Merry Christmas', it's a lyrical, intimate account of a scene, perhaps even viewed through the eyes of a child – the tone of the poetry certainly has a youthful, exuberant innocence about it. The tune itself is probably an English folk melody, possibly from Derbyshire, and while the carol was only published for the first time in the seventeenth century, it's likely that it originated early enough to be sung by sixteenth-century courtiers and countrymen.

'WE WISH YOU A MERRY CHRISTMAS'

One sixteenth-century carol we still sing enthusiastically every December is 'We Wish You a Merry Christmas'. While neither the words nor the tune are particularly outstanding, what's interesting about this catchy little carol are the customs it reveals. Both wassailing and mumming were still going strong under the Tudor monarchs, with carollers and players going from door to door performing, and it was terribly bad luck not to reward their efforts with food and drink, including the 'figgy pudding' – an early version of what we now know as Christmas pudding.

Feast Songs and Carols of Celebration

While lullabies and cradle songs were popular subjects for Tudor carols, it's much rarer to find a sacred text set to the same kind of punchy, arresting music we find in the secular works such as 'The Boar's Head Carol'. One glorious exception – perhaps the best-known Latin carol today – is 'Gaudete'.

By rights the title should have an exclamation mark after it because it's a command: 'Rejoice!' The carol poet wants everyone to celebrate because Christ is born of the Virgin Mary ('Christus est natus ex Maria virgine'). He goes on to condense the story of the incarnation very tidily into four rhyming verses, wearing some complicated scriptural ideas very lightly.

But though the poetry is sophisticated, in structure 'Gaudete' is more primitive – a proper medieval carol complete with burden, repeated not just between every verse but also at beginning and end. Listen to the difference between the verses and choruses – the verses are fast-paced, packing a lot of Latin text into a fairly short melody (just try singing a verse without tripping over your tongue), but the choruses are altogether statelier, suggesting that while the verses were intended for a soloist, everyone would have been capable of joining in with and enjoying the chorus. It's very likely that the melody predates the Tudor period, but was embellished later, its chant-like top line filled out with the fanfare-like harmonies that give the carol its kick, making it a favourite with everyone from sixteenth-century courtiers to folk-rock group Steeleye Span.

Did Henry VIII Really Write a Christmas Carol?

You can't talk about Tudor Christmas carols without at some point addressing the elephant in the room – Henry VIII and his own carol. So did the king really compose the tune 'Greensleeves' for Anne Boleyn? And if so can he really be considered the author of 'What Child is This?', the carol set to that beautiful melody?

I'm afraid that the answer, in both cases, is almost certainly no.

The popularity of 'Greensleeves' during the sixteenth century cannot be overstated – it was a hit song of its day, so well known that Shakespeare was able to reference it twice in *The Merry Wives of Windsor* without further explanation. In Act II Scene I, Mistress Ford describes Sir John Falstaff's letter of seduction in terms of the melody, arguing that the knight's manner and his words 'no more adhere and keep place together than the Hundredth Psalm to the tune of "Green Sleeves."' So, as far as Shakespeare and his contemporaries were concerned, 'Greensleeves' was definitely not a melody fit for church – it was the embodiment of all things secular and courtly, and many miles away from the carol it would later become.

If such a popular tune really had been composed by the monarch it's hard to believe that we wouldn't know it for certain – as we do with the king's other hit, 'Pastime with Good Company'. It would take a shyer king than Henry VIII to hide behind 'Anonymous' where one of the greatest melodies of his age was concerned. And then there's the question of style. Musically the tune is far more likely to date from Elizabeth I's reign than her father's, composed using the Italian *passamezzo antico* form – a sequence of chords a bit like a blues song today – not yet fashionable under Henry. Chances are, romantic though the Henry VIII story is, the tune is exactly what it sounds like – a folk song that evolved into being rather than a melody someone sat down and actively composed.

Whatever its origins though, 'Greensleeves' has a rich history. Carol writers were by no means the first to harness its tune for their own ends. Just as football fans today use well-known songs for their chants, so political and religious activists through the centuries have railed against Oliver Cromwell, Jacobites, Catholics and Puritans to this sixteenth-century tune. But eventually, in the nineteenth century, the melody found religion in the rather unlikely hands of insurance salesman William Chatterton Dix.

It was Dix who composed the words for 'What Child is This?', apparently with no particular tune in mind. It took Victorian carol compilers Reverend Henry Ramsden Bramley and Sir John Stainer to complete the journey from 'Greensleeves' to Christmas carol, bringing verse and melody together with triumphant success in their *Christmas Carols New and Old* in 1871.

But if all those facts are rather a disappointment, an anticlimax compared to the carol's more colourful myths, then let me offer some small compensation. It's quite possible that Henry VIII did write a carol after all, it just wasn't 'Greensleeves'. 'Green Grow'th the Holly' is a charming

Christmas love song, in which the author compares his enduring, unchanging love to the evergreen holly and ivy. But it adds a certain friction to the heartfelt sentiments to imagine notorious philanderer Henry VIII writing these verses.

> *Green grow'th the holly, so doth the ivy.*
> *Though winter blasts blow never so high,*
> *Green groweth the holly.*
>
> *As the holly groweth green*
> *And never changeth hue,*
> *So I am, and ever hath been,*
> *Unto my lady true.*

'MASTERS IN THIS HALL'

Although not an authentic Tudor carol, 'Masters in this Hall' does a very good job of conjuring the spirit of the sixteenth century. The words – 'Masters in this hall, hear ye news today. / Brought from over sea, and ever I you pray' – were written by none other than William Morris, the famous English textile designer, who also dabbled in poetry – very successfully. This little carol is wonderfully vigorous, especially when Morris's text is paired with its Old French dance tune. The minor key, marching pulse and angular chorus give the hearty melody a solemn edge, bringing a touch of late-medieval darkness into the brightly lit Tudor hall.

Masters in the Hall

Voice

Piano

Steady March ♩. = c.100

mf

mf

Mas - ters in this hall, hear ye news to - day.
Go - ing o'er the hills, through the milk-white snow
Shep-herds, many a one, sat a-mong the sheep
Then to Be-thle'm town, went we two by two
Ox and ass there were down on ben - ded knee
This is Christ the Lord, mas - ters be ye glad

Brought from o - ver sea and e - ver I you pray.
Heard the lambs to bleat and saw the wind to blow
No man spoke more word than they had been a - sleep
Saw the new - born babe laid in a man-ger low
Won - drous joy had I this lit - tle babe to see
Christ-mas is come in, and no man should be sad

The Birth of King's College, Cambridge

It was during the reign of Henry VIII that King's College Chapel made its first appearance in the story of Christmas. But although this magnificent building finally opened its doors for worship during the 1530s, its story, and that of King's College itself, stretches back much further. To understand the birth of this historic institution and its choir we must leave the Tudors briefly and travel back to 1441 and the reign of Henry VI.

In contrast to the worldly Henry VIII, whose love of hunting, feasting and women is well documented, Henry VI was a monarch whose Christian faith dominated his life. Wearing a hair shirt at all times under his finery, the king was so devout that he even saw the business of government as an intrusion on a life he believed should be spent in prayer, complaining, 'I can hardly snatch a moment to be refreshed by reading or any holy teaching without disturbance'.

It was these convictions that led the nineteen-year-old Henry to found King's College, Cambridge, an institution whose role he saw as helping to increase the number of clergy, 'to provide ministers of religion whose life and doctrine will give light to my subjects'. And so, on 2 April 1441, Henry himself laid the foundation stone of the college, setting in motion a project that would take almost a century to reach completion. A building such as King's College Chapel doesn't spring up overnight, but it was important to Henry that worship should not be neglected in the meantime, so a temporary chapel was built which collapsed – conveniently – almost exactly as the main college chapel was completed in 1536.

Central to Henry's plans for the college was a choir, and it wasn't enough that its members could sing. Henry's statutes of 1453 lay out in very precise terms exactly the type, number and condition of the personnel he had in mind – and they don't sound much like the choir we recognise today. First up were 16 choristers, 'poor and needy boys, of sound condition and honest conversation, being ascertainably under the age of twelve years, knowing competently how to read and sing'. In addition to their work in the chapel (and with numerous services to sing each day, those duties weren't exactly light) the choristers were expected to work in the college hall, helping the college servants 'humbly and honestly' by waiting at table.

In return for their work the boys would receive all their meals and clothing, as well as eight pence per week to go towards the cost of their board. There would also have been some musical training as well as a basic education, consisting largely of Latin grammar, some scripture and a little maths. If the boys did well under this stern regime they were given the opportunity of scholarships to King's sister institution

Eton College, and later would also be given priority if they chose to return to King's itself as students – quite a coup for boys of such poor backgrounds.

Next came six singing men, one of whom might also be called upon to play the organ. Unlike today's choral scholars these lay clerks were not members of the college, but were local professionals appointed solely for their singing ability.

But Henry's vision for King's and its chapel was rudely interrupted in 1455 by the start of the Wars of the Roses. Henry lost his crown to Edward IV, who took a dim view of a college whose loyalty remained so clearly with his rival and withdrew substantial funds. The great chapel stood, half-built, awaiting the change in fortunes that would allow it to continue its slow progress towards completion.

As battles raged across England and first Edward IV, then Richard III took charge of the nation, the college continued to ride the ever-shifting political waves, but despite Richard III's support and his edict that anyone who 'opposed or delayed' works should be imprisoned, still the chapel remained unfinished. It was only with the arrival of Henry VII that things began to change, marking a new era of certainty and support for the college.

On 22 April 1506, Henry VII attended evensong at King's. He was so impressed by the half-built chapel, so captivated by the music-making of its choir, that he pledged money for its completion, leaving his own mark on its architecture. While Henry VI had favoured stern, austere simplicity in his designs, Henry VII preferred something more lavish, and it's thanks to him that we have the many embellishments – stone carvings of Tudor roses, dragons and other exotic creatures – both inside and outside the chapel.

It wasn't all roses, however. The chapel itself may have flourished with the help of Henry VII's funds, but the choir was under new threat. In 1498, two choristers, two lay clerks and two composers were taken from King's to work in the chapel of Lady Margaret Beaufort, Henry's mother. The college wrote letters pleading for their return, but the only result was the loss of another lay clerk.

Strange though it sounds today, this horse-trading of musicians – status symbols of the day – was common practice during this period, and worked as often to King's advantage as its detriment. Under Henry VIII, royal privilege allowed the choir to claim singers from wherever they chose. In 1511 we know that singing men were 'acquired' from Norwich and Lynn, and the practice only increased through the 1530s and 1540s when choristers were brought in from across the country. Some settled into their new lives, others ran away and had to be forcibly fetched back. But it did remain a two-way process. In 1546, Master of the Chapel Royal Richard Bower paid King's a visit. He left with a chorister.

King's Chapel – a Vision Fulfilled

But despite these difficulties, King's flourished and gradually the chapel took shape. In 1536 services finally relocated

from the temporary chapel into the permanent building – one of the most magnificent and ambitious architectural projects of its kind in Europe. So what would visitors have seen as they entered this extraordinary building?

Probably the first thing to strike them then, as it still does today, is the sheer scope and scale of the chapel. Extending to 88 metres, the nave is longer than any English cathedral, drawing the eye down, past the intricately carved organ screen, to the East End where, since 1968, Rubens's *The Adoration of the Magi* has hung, warming the cool tones of the chapel with its gloriously rich autumnal colours. Next, the eye naturally drifts upwards to the intricate marvel that is the fan-vaulted ceiling. Spanning over 12 metres, the fan vault is the largest in Europe – a triumph of bold vision and ambition over practicality. It's the work of John Wastell, the last of the four masons who guided the project from foundations to its finished splendour.

Whatever time of day visitors entered the chapel, whether in daylight with the sun high in the sky or dusk as candles were lit for evensong, they couldn't help but be struck by the windows – the 12 great panels that line the nave, leading up to the East End. Deep reds and cobalt blues, vibrant greens and golds cast their jewel tones on to the stone pillars, illuminating the chapel as richly as any hand-painted manuscript of the period. How rich they must have seemed to the people of Cambridge, whose city was only now beginning to shrug off its medieval browns and greys, to swap its cramped lanes and muddy streets for something rather grander. And just as the architecture of the chapel bears witness to the many monarchs who had a hand in it, so the windows too tell the stories of changing eras and allegiances. There are hawthorn bushes to commemorate Henry VII's victory at Bosworth Field and symbols honouring Henry VIII and his wives – Anne Boleyn's falcon later quietly remodelled as a phoenix, the badge of Jane Seymour.

And then there's the acoustic. Did Henry VI and his masons know when they set about designing King's Chapel that they'd be shaping not only its architecture but its sound for centuries to come? The 'King's sound' we all know and love today is as much a product of this space – of generations of music directors responding to its demands and finding themselves blessed with its gifts – as it is the work of the singers themselves.

The chapel has about a five-second decay, meaning that any chord or note or shout takes that long to fade to nothing. It's a soft decay and a gradual one, burnishing a beautiful chord and softening its edges gently into silence. David Willcocks, director of music at King's from 1957–74 was once overheard telling a group of American tourists that the chapel acoustic was so rich, so transformatively lovely that 'It could turn a fart into a sevenfold amen'. But beware anyone singing out of tune in the chapel – the same magic that preserves the beautiful also keeps the bad hanging around, so all King's music directors have worked especially hard to keep the choral blend pure and the tuning exact. The result, dismissed by some as too precious, has an other-worldly, angelic quality – a 'halo' of sound that separates it from that of any other choir.

King's and the Reformation

As luck would have it, just as King's Chapel was finally completed and fulfilling the role its founder intended for it, the Reformation came along and changed everything.

While Henry VIII's reforms didn't greatly affect the daily life of the chapel, Edward VI's stricter edicts certainly did. The choir was disbanded altogether in 1550 and although it was later reinstated under the Catholic Mary it then had to contend with the contradictions of Elizabeth I's reign.

While officially professional church musicians were prohibited, Elizabeth's personal tastes favoured devotional music provided its textures were 'modest' and its texts 'distinct'. So King's kept its choir, but lost much of its expertise. Singers could no longer be recruited from outside Cambridge, and with much simpler music and fewer services there was little justification for the kind of skilled training that had flourished once again under Mary. By the early seventeenth century things had declined to a point where Archbishop Laud reported that 'Quiremen cannot sing and are very negligent. Choristers are half mute and come without surplices'. Even allowing for Laud's exceedingly high standards, this still paints a picture of a choir at some distance from the vision of its royal founder. It wouldn't be long before the Civil War would attack it still further, leading King's Choir into a decline that would only begin its reverse after the Restoration.

The Beginning of the End for Christmas?

Christmas too, so rosy-cheeked and overflowing with energy when we left it under Henry VIII, also began to show signs of malaise. As government became more centralised and the aristocracy traded life on their country estates for one lived increasingly at the courts of Elizabeth I and James I, the social order was changing. Without the support of old feudal structures, old traditions too began to wither – part of the past, not the future.

By the time we leave it in the seventeenth century, Christmas – beset by Puritans on one side and a growing city population on the other – was a poor shadow of its former jolly, portly self. Playwright Ben Jonson summed up the situation in *Christmas, His Masque* – a festive entertainment presented at the court of James I in 1616.

'Why, gentlemen,' cries Father Christmas, 'would you have kept me out? Christmas, old Christmas, Christmas of London, and Captain Christmas?...

I have seen the time you have wished for me, for a Merry Christmas, and now you have me, they would not let me in.'

But, like any good actor on the brink of death until tension has built sufficiently for him to recover to applause and rejoicing, Christmas and his carols weren't quite finished yet. The Victorians would soon arrive, bringing with them a passion for the festival that would give Christmas a whole new lease of life. Far from declining into nothing, Christmas celebrations would be bigger than ever and Christmas carols sung in ever greater variety and number.

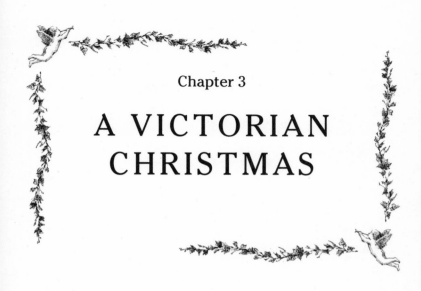

Chapter 3

A VICTORIAN CHRISTMAS

Hark the herald angels sing
'Glory to the newborn King!
Peace on earth and mercy mild
God and sinners reconciled'

(Charles Wesley, 1707–88)

So far our journey into the history of the Christmas carol has taken us through fields and woods to royal courts and even the odd alehouse, but we've barely set foot in a church. So how did we end up pious and well scrubbed, singing solemn Christian hymns along with a full congregation? The answer requires us to briefly travel back in time.

It's often said that the Victorians invented Christmas. What would perhaps be more correct to say is that they invented Christmas as we know it today – a celebration full of cards, presents, Christmas trees and carol-singing. But in their enthusiasm to seize on every festive custom they could lay their hands on and claim them for their own, they were only reacting to Christmas's history – a history they all but obliterated with their efforts.

The Puritans Cancel Christmas

Christmas in England up until the seventeenth century remained a widely celebrated winter feast, both in church – where psalms and chants were sung, and among communities – where drinking and merriment were the order of the day. The tradition of the lord of misrule (see page 38) gained popularity, bringing an anarchic quality to the celebrations. This worried the Protestant authorities, who deemed Christmas a 'popish festival with no biblical justification'. Pamphleteer Philip Stubbes painted a vivid picture of their concerns in his 1583 *The Anatomie of Abuses*.

> more mischief is that time committed than in all the year besides, what masking and mumming and whereby robbery, whoredom, murder and what not is committed? What dicing and carding, what eating and drinking, what banqueting and feasting is then used more than in all the year besides, to the great dishonour of God and impoverishing of the realm.

Seizing the opportunity to destroy a festival the Puritans saw as a dangerous mixture of pagan and Roman corruptions, a clear threat to sober Christianity, in 1642 Parliament struck the first blow, banning all Christmas plays and pageants. Then, in 1643, they went after the liturgy, banning all music in church, abolishing archbishops, bishops, choristers and vicars choral – even church organs weren't safe. In 1647 Christmas was banned altogether, replaced instead with a day of fasting – an unpopular move, but one whose shadow would prove long, stretching even beyond the Restoration in 1660.

Christmas had lost its fascination. Its holly crown had withered and even the lord of misrule's mischief couldn't entice people out to play. What was once a living and lively (often rather too lively) tradition had become something of the past – not a quaint piece of nostalgia, but an unfashionable superstition for an increasingly rational Enlightenment nation.

Eighteenth-century Gallery Choirs

But where Christmas in general sagged, carols quietly began their journey back to health and popularity. In the streets, the waits kept Christmas songs alive throughout the eighteenth century, going from house to house singing for money and beer. But it was in churches that the real changes were taking place.

The Puritans had banned all music from church, but after the Restoration it gradually returned, first in the form of psalms, then gradually hymns. As music took a more important role, churches hired choirs, first all male and later of mixed voices. Then instruments began to creep in, useful for anchoring some of the more wayward of the often untrained voices. And so West Gallery choirs were formed – so called because of the galleries many churches built for their musicians at the west end of the building. Anyone familiar with Thomas Hardy's *Under the Greenwood Tree* (1872) will remember the Mellstock Quire, exactly the kind of rustic, haphazard ensemble that was flourishing in villages across England at this time.

But what sort of carols would these local musicians have been playing? One carol we can say with absolute certainty would have been in their repertoire is 'On Ilkley Moor Baht 'At'. Well, maybe not with those words, but the melody we now associate with the song was one of the first popular folk songs to make the transition to church.

On Ilkley Moor Baht 'At

The jaunty tune (officially called 'Cranbrook' and composed by Thomas Clark) was a favourite melody for 'While Shepherds Watched' – the only Christmas hymn legally permitted to be sung in church in England for most of the eighteenth century, as its text was a paraphrase of scripture. Because of this, more melodies exist for this carol than any other, extending well into the hundreds.

But just as Hardy's musicians faced the threat from the newly fashionable organ played by Miss Fancy Day, so gallery choirs and their carols found themselves under attack from none other than the Victorians. Their crimes? Mixed forces, for one. The Victorians didn't much approve of men and women singing together. Also the sheer number of musicians. How much simpler and more efficient to replace a whole obstreperous choir with just one tame organist. And then there was the kind of noise they made; the hearty singing of men and women was fine in fields or homes, but the Victorian God, an increasingly lofty, academic sort of deity, required an altogether purer, more sexless innocence to his music-making. And so the angelic, robed choirboy was born.

'WHILE SHEPHERDS WATCHED'

The earliest carol to make it into church services, 'While Shepherds' is still sung almost entirely unchanged today. Its lyrics, though simple, are actually the work of England's sixth Poet Laureate, Nahum Tate, who for all his early success died an obscure death in a debtor's refuge in London. Although hundreds of tunes exist for Tate's popular words, the one most widely used today is called 'Winchester Old' and was written by English Tudor composer Christopher Tye – once a lay clerk at King's, Cambridge. Just imagine the reedy texture of a viol consort playing it and what might seem like a slightly dull melody takes on a much more vivid character.

The Industrial Revolution

Another threat, even greater than Victorian piety, also faced the Mellstock Quire and its ilk. The Industrial Revolution changed not only where but how people lived. Villages were decimated and families broken up as young people moved to cities. Working longer hours than ever before, they had little time or inclination to travel home for Christmas, especially when holiday was limited, and unpaid. Back in the 1790s, government workers were given a week off for Christmas, but by the 1830s this had been reduced to a single day. If the Puritans take the blame for destroying Christmas the first time round, then the Industrial Revolution was its second great threat.

But just as it seemed that Christmas and its carols were at risk of dying out altogether, the very same forces that had all but destroyed it began to fuel a revival. Increasingly isolated, living far from home in cities, people began to create their own communities, forming choral societies and gathering together with neighbours and friends to share food and company at Christmas time. Music-making exploded, fuelled by the latest accessory for every middle-class home: a piano. Industrial techniques also made printed sheet music cheaper and more accessible than ever before. Popular songs and carols were even included in the Christmas boxes sent by tradesmen to their customers.

A Carol Sheet Classic

One carol that might have appeared on these song sheets – a firm favourite throughout the nineteenth century – was the lovely 'Silent Night'. Sadly floods destroyed the tiny church of St Nikola in Oberndorf, Austria, where schoolmaster Franz Xaver Gruber and priest Joseph Mohr first performed the carol in its original German ('Stille Nacht') on Christmas Eve 1818. But though the church is gone, the legends attached to this timeless carol persist, to a point where it's hard to dig out the truth from among them.

Silent Night

It's particularly difficult to relinquish the charming tale that tells of mice chewing through vital sections of St Nikola's organ, leaving the church without music at Christmas. The resourceful young teacher and priest, so the story goes, stepped in to save the service by composing a simple carol that could be sung with just guitar accompaniment. Unfortunately facts rather get in the way of this delightful story, and even those who claim that the carol was forgotten after the original performance and only rediscovered by chance by an organ builder are almost certainly wrong.

But whatever the impetus for its composition, 'Silent Night' holds a special place for many – the inevitable winner of almost all surveys that aim to find the nation's favourite carol. Perhaps it's the infinite gentleness of the melody, or the lulling inevitability of the harmonies, or maybe it's the friction between the perfect peace the carol conjures and the brutal violence of the First World War trenches, from which soldiers from both sides famously sang the carol on Christmas Eve 1914, that speaks so powerfully to us today. For the Victorians it was almost certainly the reassuring picture the carol paints of domestic and familial bliss – the radiant young Virgin and her infant child.

Charles Dickens and Christmas

Christmas boxes and their exciting contents were just one of many new festive traditions that grew up around a revitalised Victorian festival. Christmas presents, cards, trees, crackers,

'O TANNENBAUM'

A favourite Christmas carol across the world, 'O Tannenbaum' actually makes no reference to Christmas at all. Instead the words set to this German folk song praise the fir tree with its evergreen foliage as a symbol of the enduring, the constant. Which is ironic, as the Christmas tree itself, far from a constant symbol of the festival, was a nineteenth-century innovation.

We all know the story of Queen Victoria and her German consort Albert bringing the Christmas tree to England, but in fact the young royal couple were not the first to introduce the custom. That honour goes to Queen Charlotte, George III's German wife. Missing the traditions of home, this pioneer set up the first Christmas tree at Queen's Lodge in Windsor in December 1800 – almost 50 years before Victoria and Albert would get around to it.

stockings and even Father Christmas himself were all innovations unknown before the 1830s and 1840s, and were all eagerly adopted by the growing middle classes. But while Queen Victoria and Prince Albert can take responsibility for popularising the Christmas tree and Henry Cole for the first Christmas cards, no one did more to promote the new Victorian Christmas than Charles Dickens.

The writer was so overwhelmingly associated with Christmas, that when he died a London barrow girl was apparently overheard exclaiming: 'Dickens dead? Then will Father Christmas die too?' Although many of the author's novels and short stories feature vivid Christmas scenes (*The Pickwick Papers* (1837) and 'A Christmas Dinner' (1835) in particular), it was *A Christmas Carol* that forever joined Dickens and Christmas together in the public imagination. Published on 19 December 1843, the novella was an instant success, selling 6,000 copies on Christmas Day alone.

Despite its title, however, *A Christmas Carol* features surprisingly little music. Guided by the Ghost of Christmas Present, Scrooge visits the cottage of a miner and his family.

> An old, old man and woman, with their children and their children's children, and another generation beyond that, all decked out gaily in their holiday attire. The old man, in a voice that seldom rose above the howling of the wind upon the barren waste, was singing them a Christmas song; it had been a very old

song when he was a boy; and from time to time they all joined in the chorus. So surely as they raised their voices, the old man got quite blithe and loud; and, so surely as they stopped, his vigour sank again.

We never learn the name of this 'Christmas song', but its significance is clear. Singing, whether around the piano in a middle-class parlour, or unaccompanied in the poorest of poor dwellings, brings people together. The old miner gains strength and joy in his singing from the participation of his family.

Only one carol is mentioned by name in *A Christmas Carol*, appearing at the very start of the book to provoke an as-yet-unreformed Scrooge.

The owner of one scant young nose, gnawed and mumbled by the hungry cold as bones are gnawed by dogs, stooped down at Scrooge's keyhole to regale him with a Christmas carol; but, at the first sound of—

'*God bless you, merry gentleman,*
May nothing you dismay!'

Scrooge seized the ruler with such energy of action, that the singer fled in terror, leaving the keyhole to the fog and even more congenial frost.

'God Rest Ye Merry Gentlemen' is an unusual carol in a number of ways. For a start it's in a minor key – not exactly fostering the kind of joyful, celebratory mood we expect from carols. And then there's Satan ('To save us all from Satan's power'), a far from regular character in Christmas carols, and something of a sobering presence. Both these unusual elements point to the carol's origins, not in the ribbon-wrapped world of the Victorian carol writers, but in the fifteenth century, where death and evil were much more present and accepted realities.

Despite lyrics that tell the familiar Nativity story, this carol was probably born outside the church, sung by peasants not clerics. If you listen closely, maybe even tap your fingers or clap your hands as you listen, you'll hear a dancing rhythm buried under even the more solemn of performances. It's this rhythm that betrays the carol's true origins, as a folk melody, part of the long tradition of medieval dance songs that grew up as an alternative to the darkly solemn music of the church.

Nineteenth-century Carol Collectors

'God Rest Ye Merry Gentlemen' was sung for hundreds of years before it was formally written down, but its Victorian popularity owes everything to its inclusion in *Christmas Carols New and Old*. This collection of 20 carols, published in 1867 by the Reverend Henry Ramsden Bramley and composer Sir John Stainer, fed the growing popular demand for carols, bringing many ancient ones back into circulation in elegant new arrangements, as well as introducing new ones. It's thanks to Bramley and Stainer that carols including

'THE FIRST NOWELL'

What's the most hated carol among musicians? 'The First Nowell' must surely be up there with the strongest contenders, attacked variously over the years as 'repetitive to the point of boredom', 'a terrible tune', 'a crude piece of writing' and 'second rate'. But for those of us who have a soft spot for this vigorous, hearty carol, it counts as one of Bramley and Stainer's greatest gifts to the repertoire. Stainer, though a fine composer, left us no great carols of his own, so it's his classic arrangement and harmonisation of 'The First Nowell' that is his Christmas legacy.

'The First Nowell' and 'See Amid the Winter's Snow' are still popular today.

But these two editors were only building on the work of earlier carol collectors – the true musical pioneers who had brought carols in from the cold, dusting them off and smoothing them out for a curious public. First among these was Davies Gilbert, the MP for Bodmin in Cornwall. His volume, *Some Ancient Christmas Carols*, launched the carol revival when it was published in 1822, and it was Gilbert who restored carols such as 'The First Nowell', 'A Virgin Most Pure' and 'Christians Awake' to the repertoire. His cause was taken up by William Sandys, a solicitor whose 1833 *Christmas Carols Ancient and Modern* gave us 'I Saw Three Ships' and 'Tomorrow Shall be My Dancing Day'.

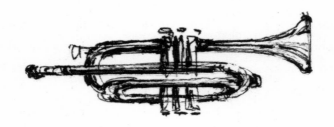

The 'Piae Cantiones'

Another rich source of Christmas carols that emerged in nineteenth-century England was the *Piae Cantiones* (*Holy Songs*). This sixteenth-century Finnish manuscript gathered together a number of medieval Latin hymns and songs, many of whose tunes we still sing today. That we know them at all is thanks to two Anglican vicars, Thomas Helmore and John Mason Neale, who between them translated the text and published the carols in new, accessible arrangements. Highlights of their *Carols for Christmas-tide* (1853) include 'Good Christian Men Rejoice', 'In Dulci Jubilo' and 'Good King Wenceslas'.

For fans of carol archaeology, anyone who loves digging the truth out from under layers of sedimented myth and legend, 'Good King Wenceslas' is a fantastic source of material. For starters, Wenceslas was neither a king, nor called Wenceslas (though he really was, by all accounts, good). Our carol hero was actually a tenth-century Bohemian duke called Vaclav, whose deeds might have been the epitome of Christian virtue and charity, but whose family was anything but. Murder was a favourite family hobby – first Vaclav's mother murdered his grandmother, and then his own brother Boleslav decided to murder his virtuous brother and steal his dukedom.

But what made nineteenth-century vicar John Neale fix on this obscure figure as the hero of his carol? Some have suggested that the 'Feast of Stephen' (Boxing Day, as we now call it) doesn't really lend itself to jollity or Christmas cheer, so Neale had to get creative when writing his lyrics. But whatever the reason, something everyone can agree on is the poor job Neale made of it.

Taking a sprightly thirteenth-century melody from the *Piae Cantiones*, originally attached to the flower carol 'Tempus Adest Floridum' ('It is Time for Flowering'), Neale wrote his own words from scratch, coming up with verses that have subsequently been dismissed as 'doggerel' and 'poor and commonplace'.

> *'Hither, page, and stand by me,*
> *If thou know'st it, telling,*
> *Yonder peasant, who is he?*
> *Where and what his dwelling?'*

DID YOU KNOW?

The 'Feast of Stephen' mentioned in 'Good King Wenceslas' is better known to us today as Boxing Day. There are many theories competing to explain the unusual name, but one gives the credit to the Victorians. This was the day on which tradesmen and servants received Christmas boxes from their employers and customers – a tip for the year's work that might include biscuits, cakes, money and small presents.

It's certainly true that the grammatical contortions Neale's language has to undergo in order to keep his rhyme scheme intact are rather awkward, but public opinion has generally overlooked this, treating the carol far more kindly than the critics. Whatever its historical inaccuracies or his poetic shortcomings, Neale's 'Good King Wenceslas' is here to stay thanks to a lively melody and a spirit of charity that spoke directly to Victorian sentimentality.

Christmas Hymns

Strictly speaking 'Good King Wenceslas' isn't a carol at all, but a hymn – a religious work deliberately composed in order to be sung in church as part of worship. It's true of most of the great carols of the late eighteenth and early nineteenth centuries – 'O Come All Ye Faithful', 'Hark! The Herald', 'Joy to the World' – none of which follow the winding, gradually evolving path of the true carol.

This growing formality is a symptom of a genre undergoing a serious rebranding exercise during this period. Just as we saw the gallery choirs with their rustic melodies and instruments replaced with organs and robed choirboys, so the music these ensembles performed also evolved. Traditional carols were smartened up in new arrangements and sometimes given new words more fitting to their sudden elevation to church, and fresh carol-hymns were composed to showcase the smart new combination of choir and organ, designed to praise God with as much splendour and soft-focus piety as any good Victorian could desire.

Classic Victorian

And so arrive some of the most famous carols – a list almost always topped by 'Hark! The Herald Angels Sing'. Curiously for a 'purpose-built' carol, 'Hark! The Herald' has gone through more adaptation and evolution than many of its folk cousins. Although hymn books tend simply to attribute the words to Charles Wesley and the melody to Felix Mendelssohn, the reality is rather more complicated, with at least five different artists involved in creating the carol as we know it today.

The story starts in 1739 with Charles Wesley, the famous poet and Methodist preacher. Walking to church one

Christmas Day, he was so entranced, so delighted, by the pealing bells that surrounded him, that he was inspired to write a hymn he called 'Hark How All the Welkin Rings'. At least two fellow preachers (George Whitefield and later Martin Madan) took issue with Wesley's verse – written, as usual, in a hurry – and made changes, most importantly getting rid of the affected and archaic 'welkin' (meaning the sky or heavens) and giving us the first line as we know it today, 'Hark! The herald angels sing'.

The tune is another composite job and if it weren't for the nineteenth century doing its bit to improve on the original then the carol might never have achieved anything like the popularity it has today. The carol's original melody was probably the tune called 'Easter Hymn', best known with Wesley's words 'Christ the Lord is Risen Today'. But it was an awkward marriage between verse and music, and in 1855 English organist William Cummings had the inspired idea of fitting Wesley's text instead to music by Mendelssohn – the *Festgesang* (*Festival Song*), composed to celebrate the 400th anniversary of Gutenberg's invention of moveable type. So it was a long journey, involving three poets, three musicians and over a century of editing, but eventually this unusual march-style carol found its feet and hasn't looked back since.

Carols Cross the Atlantic

America, still a young country and keen to create traditions of its own during this period, was another source of memorable

Christmas hymns. One of the loveliest, 'It Came Upon the Midnight Clear', was written as the snow fell outside, one cold December day in 1849.

> *It came upon the midnight clear,*
> *That glorious song of old,*
> *From angels bending near the earth,*
> *To touch their harps of gold:*
> *'Peace on the earth, goodwill to men,*
> *From heaven's all-gracious King.'*
> *The world in solemn stillness lay,*
> *To hear the angels sing.*

The Reverend Edmund Hamilton Sears was a Massachusetts minister newly returned to his parish after serious illness. While recuperating at home, he was inspired to write verses that speak as eloquently of his own nation and time as they do of the birth of Jesus. The hymn sets up a conflict between the songs of the angels, bringing a message of peace and goodwill from the heavens, and the conflict on earth below – so noisy that men are deaf to the music above them.

> *Yet with the woes of sin and strife*
> *The world has suffered long;*
> *Beneath the angel-strain have rolled*
> *Two thousand years of wrong;*

And man, at war with man, hears not
The love-song which they bring:
O hush the noise, ye men of strife,
And hear the angels sing.

For Sears, writing as the tensions of the Civil War were already brewing, the idea of 'man at war with man' needed little imagination. It's a poignant image that has lost none of its immediacy in the conflicts of our own century.

Musically, how you sing this carol rather depends on where in the world you are singing it. If you're American, you'll be enjoying Richard Storrs Willis's deliciously lilting 6/8 melody, a beautiful piece of writing that manages to capture both the wistful nostalgia and the quiet hopefulness of the lyrics. If you're English though, it's much more likely that you'll be singing Sears's words in the rather more four-square setting by Arthur Sullivan (he of Gilbert and Sullivan fame). Sullivan himself adapted it from an older English melody and the result is fairly pedestrian, except for a glorious sun-emerging-from-behind-clouds moment in the last two lines of each verse as we move back into the major.

'Joy to the World'

Hugely popular in America, where it remains one of the most-published carols of all time, 'Joy to the World' has become American by association and adoption. But the

It Came Upon the Midnight Clear

carol's parentage is actually rather more complicated. The words are definitely English (sorry America), written in 1719 by 'the bard of Southampton' Isaac Watts, a priest and prolific author of hymns. But here things start to get mysterious.

About a century after the carol lyrics first appeared, the carol was published with a rousing, ear-catching tune simply marked 'from Handel'. However, no musical source has ever been found and most likely the melody is actually the work of Lowell Mason, an American whose passion for the composers of the past may have allowed more than a little Handel to creep into his work – hence the slightly apologetic attribution. But whatever its source, 'Joy to the World' remains one of the most ebullient and outright ecstatic of all carols – a transatlantic meeting of minds that's well worth fighting over.

Carols for Children

While medieval carol lyrics tend to call a spade a spade, valuing directness and simplicity above all things, Victorian carols prefer a rather softer, more euphemistic approach. It's an approach reflected in fashions right across the period, from clothes to language itself, but is nowhere clearer than in attitudes towards children.

In previous centuries, when lives were shorter and more precarious, children were part of the workforce from an early age, exposed to the same hardships and cruel realities as their parents. But thanks partly to the Industrial Revolution and its new urban population (for the first time children weren't going out into the fields to work) and partly also to newly fashionable evangelical doctrines, children were now seen as their own species – precious, innocent and in need of guidance and protection.

And so the educational carol was born. The success of Mrs C.F. Alexander's *Hymns for Little Children* (1848) – home of hymns such as 'All Things Bright and Beautiful' – shows the huge market that children suddenly represented, and it's thanks to this youthful new congregation that we have Christmas classics such as 'Away in a Manger' and 'O Little Town of Bethlehem'. Both, as it happens, are American, and both also hail from Philadelphia.

'Away in A Manger'

For so sweet and uncomplicated a carol, 'Away in a Manger' has certainly had its fair share of controversy. First there was the authorship scandal (well, maybe not a scandal exactly, but certainly a heated debate). When the carol was first published in 1884 it was under the title of 'Luther's Cradle Song'. The accompanying text stated for a fact that Martin Luther composed the carol, and it took well over 50 years for this myth to be satisfactorily debunked. Because while Luther certainly wrote his fair share of hymns, this wasn't among them.

Then there was the problem of music. The original editors published the carol without a melody of its own, suggesting instead that the words be sung to the popular tune 'Home! Sweet Home!'. But the temptation to improve on an already popular carol was huge and many composers tried their hand at setting the words (today almost 50 potential tunes have been identified). The one that has stuck, however, and the one we all grow up singing is by Pennsylvania schoolmaster William James Kirkpatrick – an attractive melody, whose gently rocking rhythms give this cradle song its character.

But critics weren't quite done with the carol yet. Yet another controversy has raged around the seemingly innocuous line, 'But little Lord Jesus, no crying He makes'. To some, this claim suggests that the infant Jesus is not fully human – a heresy that others, with equal vehemence, have of course denied.

'O Little Town of Bethlehem'

Less contentious but no less loved, 'O Little Town of Bethlehem' is a rare Victorian carol inspired not by the snowy Christmas landscapes of Northern Europe and America, but by an authentic Middle Eastern scene. In December 1865 the young Episcopalian pastor Phillips Brooks left his Philadelphia parish to travel to the Holy Land. What he saw there struck him so profoundly that, three years later, its images coalesced into a beautiful carol in which he imagines looking down over the lights of Bethlehem one night from a nearby hill.

> *O little town of Bethlehem,*
> *How still we see thee lie!*
> *Above thy deep and dreamless sleep*
> *The silent stars go by.*
> *Yet in thy dark streets shineth*
> *The everlasting Light;*
> *The hopes and fears of all the years*
> *Are met in thee tonight.*

But while Brooks's lyrics were written at leisure, the same cannot be said of the original melody. Brooks had asked the organist at his church, Lewis Redner, to come up with a tune for his melody, but Redner had procrastinated so long that the carol very nearly missed Christmas altogether. But the angels were clearly having none of it, and on Christmas

Eve Redner found himself suddenly awake with a musical 'gift from heaven' haunting his ears. He wrote it down, and the result, 'St. Louis', has become a favourite tune for Americans.

A little high in sentimental sugar content for English congregations, however, the tune was discarded by Vaughan Williams when he came to edit *The English Hymnal* in 1906. It was replaced with a solid home-grown folk melody called 'Forest Green' that he himself had collected on a summer's day in Surrey from an elderly villager called Mr Garman.

King's During the Nineteenth Century

The nineteenth century wasn't just a high point in the evolution of carols, it was also the era in which King's College Choir became the professional ensemble we know today – transformed almost singlehandedly by the efforts of the college's longest-serving and much-loved organist Arthur Henry Mann.

But before Mann arrived in 1876 to revive the choir's fortunes, it had to survive the downturn of the previous hundred years. It's unclear quite what caused the decline in standards – both of music and general welfare among the choristers – but by the 1830s things were thoroughly Dickensian. Choristers were still chosen, according to Henry VI's original statutes, from among poor local boys, but the results were challenging.

In order to be appointed a chorister, boys needed only
to prove they could write their name, address and age as
well as sing a scale in tune. Life at King's College School
was tough. Lunch consisted of a single slice of meat and
bread (vegetables made only the rarest of appearances)
and the senior choristers, whose roles still included
waiting in the college hall, often stole morsels of food
to supplement it. But each chorister was allowed a daily

half pint of beer, and each December after the ceremonial fitting of a new top hat and gown the choristers would head to the Hat and Feathers pub and consume 'a large quantity of ale'!

Bullying was rife among the boys (a favourite trick involved propelling a new chorister over the wall into Clare College's Fellows' Garden in order to find the mythical blue rabbits and then abandoning him to the wrath of the gardener with no means of escape) and schoolroom teaching and discipline so rough that when two fellows of the college witnessed conditions in 1842 they immediately began a campaign for reform.

An Act of Parliament passed in 1856 permitted King's to rewrite its statutes and at last the college and its choristers were allowed to move into a new era. Better terms were offered to potential choristers in an attempt to recruit a better class of boy and grants introduced to help with the boys' musical and academic education. Most importantly, proper provision was made for lodging boys – the first step towards the boarding school that would eventually be established.

The professional 'singing men', the lay clerks who still formed the back rows of the choir, also presented something of a problem. Standards of singing were low, with no way of dismissing those not up to the task, and rehearsals haphazard at best. Absenteeism and insubordination were also the norm and any attempts to address this were complicated by the fact that each singer was employed not only at King's but also at Trinity College.

'Daddy' Mann

That all changed in 1876 when the college persuaded music director William Amps to retire and appointed Mann in his stead. It was Mann who opened up choristerships to boys from outside Cambridge and also introduced the idea of choral scholars – students of the college who would sing as part of the choir during their time at King's – to replace the increasingly elderly and problematic lay clerks. The process was a gradual one (the final lay clerk only departed in 1928), but paved the way for a properly professional ensemble of much higher quality.

A boarding school was established, which though primitive (lacking heating, hot water or any sort of recreational facilities) was clean and serviceable, and a new set of chorister rules established in 1880 helped formalise the status and responsibilities of the boys. Choristers were forbidden to visit the rooms of any college member without special permission, and also from accepting any presents from them. They could no long 'loiter about the courts of the college or the streets' or wander out of bounds. They also had to pass the annual examination, or else risk losing their choristerships.

The 26-year-old Mann brought with him not only energy and reforming zeal, but also a passion for the music of his Victorian contemporaries – something he clung to throughout his time at the college, long after such repertoire and old-fashioned style of performance had fallen out of fashion. But under his care the choir flourished and for the first time the public was allowed to witness their music-making (prior to this any visitor who wished to attend a service needed a written order from a college fellow). It was Mann who first established what has become 'the King's sound' – a rich, sonorous style of singing adapted to suit the chapel's generous acoustic, and frequently coloured with dramatic crescendos and diminuendos. Mann's own organ playing also tended to the lush, to the despair of certain college fellows who longed for something a little more sprightly and who worked hard to persuade him to broaden his tastes.

Mann would stay at King's until his death in 1929, an astonishing 53-year reign that saw the choir move from a world of high-Victorian pomp to the twentieth century – though surprisingly little changed, as choristers from the end of his time recall. Patrick Magee, a chorister from 1924–8, paints a vivid picture of his arrival at King's.

Arrayed in stiff collar and short Eton jacket, striped trousers and top-hatted, I entered King's College School. There were forty-seven boys in those far days (now there are over three hundred), presided over by Mr C.R. Jelf, a schoolmaster of almost Dickensian proportions, complete with wing collar, button boots, bowler hat and everything else in tone. My memory of the school is that it was always cold in winter, for warmth would be considered bad for health and even more so for character. I can still see Mr Jelf stooping down to extinguish those slender gas heaters as the temperature rose much above fifty degrees – if ever it did. [Highlands and Lowlands, Patrick Magee, unpublished memoir – written permission given by exeucutor]

Magee's contemporary David Briggs – the only surviving chorister to have been directed by Mann – has similar memories.

Life at the school was quite spartan, very simple. I think our fees were only eight pounds per term, and it was quite tough actually. There wasn't an awful lot of heating or that sort of thing. It took great quantities of rice pudding to keep us going. But it was an unforgettable experience.

But for both Magee and Briggs the dominant memory of their life at King's, the 'real life and soul' of the place was

'Daddy' Mann. To this day, Briggs still has a photo of the organist above his bed, remembering him as a 'profoundly religious man' who he and all the other boys 'absolutely adored'.

Kind and sensitive to all around, infinitely gentle to any chorister or choral scholar in personal difficulty, Mann was also a perfectionist who would accept nothing less than the best – as Magee explains.

> Dr Mann conducted the choir with complete professionalism; no member got away with a sloppy lead, impure tuning or a wrong note. An occasion is recorded when an evensong did not meet with his approval and a message was sent that the men and boys were required to assemble in the stalls. Mounting the dais his only comment was 'You can do better than that' and the choir was made to sing through the whole service again, Mann standing with an expression as of the Last Judgement. At the end of this he walked out without saying a word.

But, in general, life for the choir and its choristers became joyful, especially at Christmas time, when treats and practical jokes added colour to the choir's routine. The dean's party was an annual highlight, and choristers learned to beware teaspoons that would collapse without warning, revealing a hidden hinge, and squeaking cream buns. Best of all was the Pandemonium Harp – a small wooden cigar box with a tin of water concealed within it. New choristers were invited to try and play it by blowing down the pipes that extended vertically upwards, propelling the water with considerable force into their own eyes, much to the delight of all onlookers.

'Once in Royal David's City'

When we think of A.H. Mann and his time at King's, there's one Christmas carol more than any other that comes to mind – a symbol of this generous, passionate musician and his musical legacy: 'Once in Royal David's City'. Not only is it the iconic King's carol – the annual start of Christmas and the service of Nine Lessons and Carols – but it's Mann's own 'remarkable' harmonisation that gives the carol its identity, making it the glorious processional work we know and love today.

So timeless is the opening of King's Nine Lessons and Carols – the solo treble, that rising musical phrase emerging out of silence – that it's hard to believe it was ever any other way. But the very first service, on Christmas Eve 1918, started not with 'Once in Royal' but the altogether perkier 'Up! Good Christen Folk'. It was an experiment that was never to be repeated. By the service's second year 'Once in Royal' had taken its place, where it would remain, becoming as important a part of the service's architecture as the final lesson from St John's Gospel.

In many ways, 'Once in Royal' is the typical nineteenth-century carol. Tender (some might even say saccharine), wide-eyed and sweetly earnest, it won't come as much of a surprise to learn that it was written by a bishop's wife (or soon-to-be-wife), Cecil Frances Alexander (see page viii), one of the most successful writers of her generation and author of the unassumingly titled *Hymns for Little Children*. Published in 1848, this slim volume of devotional verses proved so popular that by the end of the century the book was on its astonishing 69th edition. Big hits from the book included 'All Things Bright and Beautiful', 'There is a Green Hill Far Away' and, of course, 'Once in Royal'.

Intended as an educational tool, designed to introduce children to Christian values and the story of the Nativity in simple, direct language, the verse is nothing very special. But when, a year after its publication, English organist Henry John Gauntlett came across it and set Alexander's words to music, the result was a carol that has become so much greater than the sum of its parts. But how?

Some point to the quiet grandeur of Mann's harmonisation, taking something simplistic and giving it musical weight and scope; others to the charming, folk-style simplicity of Gauntlett's melody. But perhaps the magic of this very special carol is that shared by all the greatest vocal or choral works – the alchemy that happens when words meet music that not only echoes but also amplifies them. Here, Alexander's touching emphasis not on Christ as saviour and defender but as a baby, a helpless infant so familiar and fragile, meets Mann's innovation of the solo treble. To open a great festal service not with a musical bang but a whimper is as powerful as it is true both to the spirit of Christmas and the Festival of Nine Lessons and Carols itself. For all their excess, their sentimentality and their often questionable taste, the Victorians certainly knew a thing or two about carols.

A Timeline of King's Chapel

1446　The foundation stone of the chapel is laid by Henry VI

1461　Foundations of the chapel are completed

1477　Plans for the roof change from a simple design to ambitious fan vaulting

1506　Henry VII visits and grants funds to allow construction to continue

1512　The chapel's basic shell is completed and roofed in timber and lead

1515　The chapel's fan vaulting is finished after just three years' work

1531　The stained-glass windows are completed and installed

1536　The organ screen and wooden panelling are installed

1536　Temporary chapel collapses and services move into the permanent chapel

King's by Numbers

- King's Choir was founded 575 years ago in 1441
- Choir is made up of 16 choristers and 14 choral scholars
- Choristers range in age from 9 to 13
- The choir has had only 15 music directors since 1606
- The choir sings 7 services each week for 24 weeks of the year
- The choir gets 1 day off each week – Monday
- The choir have made over 100 recordings

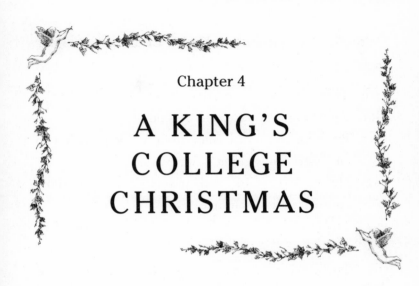

Chapter 4

A KING'S COLLEGE CHRISTMAS

Silent night, holy night,
all is calm, all is bright
round yon virgin mother and child.
Holy infant, so tender and mild,
sleep in heavenly peace,
sleep in heavenly peace.

(Joseph Mohr, 1792–1848)

Christmas Eve 1914 was, by all accounts, a cold night. Damp had turned to frost along much of the Western Front, veiling the bodies strewn across no man's land in a white shroud. Men on both sides, wearied and wounded by battles at Namur, Marne, Antwerp and, of course, Ypres, longed for respite from a war no one now believed would be 'over by Christmas'.

Suddenly lights pricked the darkness around the German trench and a sound broke the silence. Distant, indistinct at first, it gradually coalesced into melody and meaning. 'Stille Nacht! Heilige Nacht! / Alles schläft; einsam wacht'. The language may have been alien, but both the carol and its intent were unmistakeable.

As the final verse faded away the British soldiers took up the song, answering the Germans with a hearty rendition of 'The First Nowell'. The musical dialogue continued, passing back and forth until finally the British broke into 'O Come All Ye Faithful'. Immediately they felt their voices swell; joining in from the opposite trench were the German soldiers, singing the carol to its original Latin words, 'Adeste fideles...'.

The story of the Christmas truce is a familiar one – a legend embellished and embroidered with time, but one with its origins in the muddy, bloody facts of the First World War. It's in these same trenches that the Festival of Nine Lessons and Carols has its roots. The instinct that drove thousands of soldiers, spread hundreds of miles along the length of the front line, to exchange silence for song that Christmas Eve is also that which propelled a young army chaplain to create a service that has gone on to inspire not only his own generation, but all those that have followed since: a yearning for peace, reconciliation, consolation from horror and, above all, beauty.

You only have to read Eric Milner-White's Bidding Prayer – the beautiful words that have been spoken during the Festival of Nine Lessons and Carols every year since 1919 – to see both where the service comes from and where it directs its hopeful gaze. We may anticipate with delight the 'message of the angels', leading us ultimately to 'the Babe lying in a manger', but do so in full knowledge and acceptance of 'all those who rejoice with us, but upon another shore and in a greater light, that multitude which no man can number'. In 1919, in a college that had lost so many of its own to the conflict, those words must have pierced even as they consoled.

The Man Who Brought Carols to King's

But who was Eric Milner-White, the 'very, very shy, but tremendously kind' 34-year-old cleric responsible for shaping the service of Nine Lessons and Carols into the form we know today? Born in 1884 to upper-middle-class parents in Southampton, an education at Harrow took Milner-White to King's on a scholarship. He left with a double first in history. A career in academia or education beckoned, but Milner-White instead joined the Church, taking up his first appointment in London in 1908. It was here that real-world experience – knowledge gained from the people he would encounter in his slum parishes in Elephant and Castle and Woolwich – was first added to his religious convictions, sowing seeds that would eventually flower in his later career into liturgy designed for simplicity and broad appeal.

In 1912 Milner-White returned to King's as chaplain,
but the appointment was abruptly cut short in August 1914
by the declaration of war. The young man immediately
volunteered and by December had traded the stillness
and beauty of King's Chapel for the noise, brutality and
squalor of the French front line – the life of an army
chaplain. Few of Milner-White's letters from this period

survive (he destroyed many in later life), so we are largely left to imagine the horror such an environment must have represented for a man of his compassion and social conscience.

One letter does survive, however. Dated 15 June 1915 and written to King's provost M.R. James (familiar to many as the father of the contemporary ghost story), it gives a vivid picture of the violence even Milner-White, as a non-combatant, faced daily.

> [Battle] is indescribable, unimaginable. The fresh night air was itself a rushing road like a waterfall, as a thousand shells tore through it. The dark blue sky was lit up by a summer lightning flash upward from the earth every second...The continuous firework of light balls went up from the German trenches. But most awesome was the noise. We felt so powerless against those splitting cracks and roars, and dreamt of the metal tearing its way into the bodies of poor men.[1]

Returning to King's once again in 1918, now as the newly-appointed dean of the college, Milner-White turned his attention to a question he had begun to grapple with while in France. Faced with the daily horrors of the front, the daily invasion of death into life, he felt increasingly dissatisfied with the Anglican liturgy, finding it not just inadequate but actively irrelevant to the needs of his men, an issue on which he clashed openly with Chaplain-General John Taylor Smith. Back in Cambridge he continued to explore these same questions of relevance, accessibility and usefulness, reassessing the needs of a college chapel and coming to some potentially provocative conclusions. For a start, he refused to consider any return to enforced worship for the students, acknowledging that:

> Any form of compulsory chapel is going to be hard after the war...The falling off in the numbers of undergraduates at morning service on Sunday does not distress me...Under present day conditions it seems inevitable.

The extent of his reforming ambitions is clear from a memo to M.R. James, in which Milner-White outlines King's unique position among Church institutions.

> I suggest that in the matter of public worship, no Church in the land is more fitted than ours to take the lead. We are free from the ecclesiastical authority which governs even the most 'live' cathedrals. We have, I hope, both the learning and the sober sense which will prevent the extravagances either of ignorance or of one-sided enthusiasms...We have unrivalled musical resources.[2]

One particular focus of Milner-White's reforms was the chapel's 'Occasional Services' – seasonal celebrations such as Holy Week, Advent and, of course, Christmas – where creativity and innovation could most effectively be applied. Here, for the first time, we see the Festival of Nine Lessons and Carols begin to take shape. Milner-White's vision of 'Colour, warmth and delight' placed aesthetic concerns to the fore with simple beauty and spiritual truth, appealing to a generation disillusioned with faith and hardened by war.

The Birth of Nine Lessons and Carols

Milner-White wasn't working from scratch. Tempting though it is to think of the Festival of Nine Lessons and Carols coming to life in the splendour of King's Chapel, framed by the Gothic fan vaulting and the intricately carved rood screen, its birth – appropriately, for a Christmas service – was an altogether humbler affair. The very first service of Nine Lessons and Carols in 1880 was held not in a church or chapel but a wooden hut – the temporary 'wooden cathedral' of Truro.

The original author of the service was Edward White Benson, the first bishop of Truro. Taking on a brand-new diocese, created in 1876, he inherited neither traditions nor a cathedral in which to house them, and immediately set about creating both. While John Loughborough Pearson was building the splendid new Gothic Revival cathedral, all services were housed in a small wooden hut nearby. Lacking heating and much by way of ventilation, it must have been a devoted congregation indeed who spent seven years worshipping there.

True to the tradition of carols themselves, Benson's service of Nine Lessons and Carols did not spring fully formed, but was itself an organic evolution of earlier customs. An old practice of singing Christmas carols in the streets of Truro in the lead-up to the festival first became formalised in 1878, when Benson's succentor George Walpole decided that something was needed on Christmas Eve, 'both as a counter-attraction to the public houses and as a right prelude to Christmas.'[3] That first carol service proved a success and gained scope the following year when it became a festal service, its carols enriched by prayers, lessons and a sermon.

It was Bishop Benson who took this service and gave it the shape that endures today, taking inspiration for his creation from medieval traditions for celebrating feast days. Benson's son Arthur writes in his biography of Edward:

> My father arranged from ancient sources a little
> service for Christmas Eve. Nine carols and nine tiny
> lessons...were read by various officers of the church,
> beginning with a chorister, and ending, through the
> different grades, with the Bishop.[4]

In this way, Benson created what Milner-White would later describe as 'the two most important contributions to the service as we know it', the sequence of lessons, and the hierarchical sequence of readers, moving from least important to most important. Together they provided a skeleton structure on which Milner-White himself would later build.

History doesn't relate precisely how Milner-White came to hear of the Truro service, whether through M.R. James (a great friend of Bishop Benson's son, who had spent Christmas with the family in Truro in 1882) or more directly from Arthur Benson himself. But whatever the process, in 1918, just six weeks after the end of the Great War, Milner-White introduced his own variant to King's for the first time.

The order of service for that first Christmas Eve experiment was substantial, not to say ponderous. Although Milner-White did away with the choruses from Handel's *Messiah* favoured by Benson, feeling them ill-suited to the occasion, he kept almost all of the bishop's other elements. In addition to the sequence of nine readings and nine carols that we know today, there were no fewer than five congregational hymns, a sung setting of the 'Magnificat' by Charles Wood and a sequence of spoken benedictions. As Milner-White himself later admitted, 'The Bishop's scheme, excellent on paper, did not transfer so well into action.'[5]

MUSIC FOR 1918 FESTIVAL OF NINE LESSONS AND CAROLS AT KING'S

Invitatory Carol: 'Up! Good Christen Folk'

Hymn: 'Once in Royal David's City'

Hymn: 'A Great and Mighty Wonder'

Carol: 'A Virgin Most Pure'

Carol: 'Blessed be that Maid Marie'

Carol: 'As Up the Wood I Took My Way'

Hymn: 'While Shepherds Watched'

Carol: 'Unto Us is Born a Son'

Hymn: 'O Come All Ye Faithful'

Carol: 'O Night, Peaceful and Blest'

Carol: 'Childing of a Maiden Bright'

Carol: 'In Dulci Jubilo'

Carol: 'The First Nowell'

'Magnificat'

Recessional Hymn: 'Hark! The Herald Angels Sing'

But these 'blemishes', as Milner-White called them, were largely ironed out the following year and the 1919 service remains the model from which subsequent years have scarcely deviated. Here, for the first time, 'Once in Royal David's City' took its place as the first hymn, although sung for the first few years by all the choristers rather than as a solo, and the sequence of readings was rearranged to give a more satisfying arc. Most significantly, perhaps, the ninth lesson from Galatians was replaced with the story of the Incarnation from St John's Gospel – the reading that has remained the spiritual and emotional climax of the service ever since.

It's easy to be beguiled by the rich, emotive variety of the carols and by the beautiful singing of King's Choir into forgetting that it is the lessons, not the music, that form the unchanging core of the Festival of Nine Lessons and Carols. It was something that Milner-White himself, for all his emphasis on the aesthetic side of the service, felt very strongly about.

> Their liturgical order and pattern is the strength of the service, and prevents it becoming a recital of carols rather than an act of worship. For it is fatally easy to weaken and ruin the devotion, to make it mere community carol singing, by reducing the number of Lessons and doubling the number of carols.[6]

It is this biblical narrative, moving from Old Testament to New, from Creation to Incarnation, that guides us through the service, inspiring the carols that grow out of each lesson, commenting on and enriching them through music and poetry. The service begins with the fall of man in the Garden of Eden, before turning to a message of hope in God's promise to Abraham, Isaiah's prophecies of the birth of Jesus and of a second Eden. We then turn to the Christmas story itself, moving from the Annunciation through the journey to Bethlehem, the shepherds and the Wise Men, to climax in the mystery of the Incarnation. The strength of the service is its simplicity, its faith in the texts and the music – allowing each to tell their story directly to the listening congregation without the gloss or intermediary of a sermon.

To Milner-White's colleagues it must have seemed radical indeed. Even M.R. James, a long-standing supporter of the young dean, expressed his doubts about the Festival of Nine Lessons and Carols, only to have them dissolved by the potent experience of the 1918 service. We mustn't forget that James, like many at King's, remembered the beauty of the old evensong-based Christmas Eve service. It's thanks to James that we have what is arguably the most atmospheric description anyone has yet written of Christmas Eve at King's. What he describes is not, in fact, the service of Nine Lessons and Carols, but what he captures in his prose is precisely the essence of Milner-White's creation.

> We of the college surpliced ourselves and repaired to chapel. Choir and ante-chapel were full and dark. Just before the clock struck five the boys would issue from their vestry on the north side, the men from the Hacombleyan chantry on the south; ... A faint musical hum was heard, of the choir taking up the note, and then – it seemed to give the very spirit of Christmas – the boys broke quite softly into 'Once In Royal David's City' and began moving eastward. With the second verse the men joined in. I declare I do not know what has moved me more than this, and still does when I recall it.[7]

Word of the new service spread quickly beyond the college and as early as 1919 the *Cambridge Daily News* mentions the 'very large number' attending Nine Lessons and Carols at King's. By 1921, just three years after its inception, the service had become part of the fabric of city life, a regular fixture of the year, with the same paper reporting that 'King's College Chapel, as usual, was packed for the carol service.'

But Milner-White's legacy to King's did not end with his Christmas service. His role as dean brought with it responsibilities in the choir school, and in these this shy man found a natural outlet for his kindness, energy and sense of fun. The awkwardness that often afflicted him in the company of adults, especially women, melted away in the easy interaction of children, and whether teaching scripture to the senior boys, playing riotous games of cricket on Sunday nights or in the confirmation classes he held in his college rooms (complete with tea and buns), he quickly established himself as a favourite teacher.

The best and most vivid memories of Milner-White all come, however, from outside term time. Every August between 1921 and 1939 the dean ran a camp at Batcombe in Somerset for all choristers, ex-choristers, choral scholars and undergraduates training for the priesthood. Nearly 300 boys attended over the years, all revelling in the outdoor life of camping, sports, cycling outings to nearby towns and churches, and campfire singing in the evenings. It was a magical world and one where the young choristers – so busy and professional during the school year – could really relax and be children.

First Radio Broadcast

For the first decade of its life, Milner-White's Festival of Nine Lessons and Carols remained a local phenomenon, a 'gift to the City of Cambridge'. But that all changed in 1928 with the first radio broadcast of the service, by the BBC. It wasn't the first service to be broadcast from King's Chapel, that honour goes to an evensong in 1926, but it was the service that caught the imagination of a nation like no other before it.

Yet the service arrived in the BBC schedules without fanfare. A quick glance through the *Radio Times* for December 1928 finds only a small notice of the programme at the bottom of a page, tucked between advertisements for Bovril ('Increase Your Bovrility'), Veno's Lightning Cough Cure and Hovis ('Every Round a Square Meal'). It reads: 'Christmas Eve, the day of carols, will be celebrated by carol singing from King's College Cambridge, and from the churchyard of Whitechapel Parish Church.'[8]

The same surprisingly matter-of-fact tone permeates the journal of Patrick Magee, the senior chorister of King's Choir in 1928 and later a chaplain of the college, when he recalls this historic first broadcast. The thirteen-year-old Magee writes: 'Christmas Eve. Practice 10–12.45. Go out to dinner with Mum and Dad. Carol service broadcasted [sic]. Comes off well. I read a lesson and sing a solo in "Lullay".'[9]

And yet the technical challenges of transmitting a service live from a space like King's with its notoriously difficult acoustic must have been an almost impossibly ambitious feat in 1928, involving early Marconi-Reisz microphones slung on cables across the chapel as well as fixed around the building. David Briggs, the only surviving chorister from that first Nine Lessons and Carols broadcast remembers 'one occasion where the crucifix actually collided with the microphone which was hanging from the ceiling'. But that, and all other issues, were calmly and efficiently dealt with by 'A chap called Mr Anderson, who used to come year after year from the BBC with a box of tricks that he would unpack in the vestry.' Indeed, it was the same Mr Anderson who ensured the successful broadcast of the service on the BBC for many decades to come.

With one exception. In 1930 no Christmas Eve service was broadcast from King's – the only gap in an otherwise unbroken history of nearly a century. Why the omission?

Theories (conspiracy and otherwise) abound, but there are several plausible reasons for the gap. Perhaps the most likely involves the acoustic challenges of King's itself – a theory supported by a BBC press release of 1958.

> In 1929, [...]there was no intention of putting it on the air every year; indeed difficulties with the acoustic militated against a complete radio success. In 1930 it was dropped by the BBC but next year the broadcasts were resumed – the awkward acoustics which give King's some of its special characters having been got under control.[10]

Other possibilities include: the theory that King's Boris Ord, the still very new director of music, was not yet deemed a sufficiently safe pair of hands for so high profile a broadcast; and the suggestion that the BBC's new broadcasting policy for religious programming led to an impasse with Milner-White. But whatever the truth of the matter, by 1931 the difficulty had been overcome and the broadcast was allowed to return – this time for good – and by 1938 *The Times* was hailing the service as 'the most lovely annual event of the year, and one of those most appreciated by listeners.'[11]

The value of the service only increased through the 1930s. In 1938 the first American broadcast of the service was transmitted by the Mutual Broadcasting System, and networks in Italy, France and Switzerland also took portions of the relay, as well as – of course – the BBC World Service, ensuring an ever-wider congregation for Milner-White's creation. During the Second World War these broadcasts continued (though their source location was kept anonymous until after transmission), used as morale boosters for British troops, and reaching not only Switzerland and France but even Belgium, Holland and Czechoslovakia.

An article from the December 1954 *Radio Times* gives some insight into the emotional value and meaning the service held for people during the war years.

> In several German prisoner-of-war camps carol services with Lessons were held. At the Opera House of Caserta in Italy an Anglo-American choir of troops sang carols, and the Lessons were read in a series starting with a private, ending with a general. In a Japanese prisoner-of-war camp the curtain rose on a scene representing a room at the BBC. An announcer said 'We are taking you to King's'; then it rose again on two rows of prisoners, dressed in white costumes, meant to look like surplices, and singing carols to the accompaniment of camp-made instruments. 'It sounded,' said my informant, 'something like Ord'.[12]

The People's Service

King's Festival of Nine Lessons and Carols has always attracted a large congregation, filling the chapel to absolute capacity. But with the international reach of the radio and television broadcasts has come an unwelcome celebrity. The service has become a victim of its own success, with hundreds of people desperate to attend each year. The college could quite easily issue or even sell tickets, but true to the spirit of what remains a service and not a public concert, they operate an entirely democratic system. Anyone who is prepared to come and queue early enough on the morning of Christmas Eve will get a place in the chapel.

The result is that each year, several days before the service, a queue begins to form outside the college lodge. At first it's only one or two die-hard enthusiasts determined to get the very best seats up in the choir, but as Christmas Eve draws closer it begins to swell. People come from all over the world to hear the choir they've known from the radio or television for so many years. Some bring their children or come with friends, ex-choristers come and meet up with their friends, and there's a real party atmosphere. The choral scholars help, serenading the queue each year – no matter how bad the weather – with carols and close-harmony arrangements.

Someone who knows the process better than anyone else, who's almost as much a part of Christmas Eve at King's as the choir themselves, is Ian de Massini. Massini has queued every year since 1976, making 2016 his fortieth consecutive service. After initially camping out in the queue for just a single night, Massini has now extended what he calls his annual 'pilgrimage' into three days and nights – a process that's become very special to him.

> I use the first two days and nights before other people arrive to meditate – to close my eyes, focus and slow down in preparation for the service itself. I do bring books, but I never read them, although I sometimes listen to Radio 3. I've perfected my kit over the years and don't get cold. Basically as long as you've got a camp bed, some thermals and a sleeping bag you're fine. That being said, I do live close enough so that if the weather gets really bad I can dash back to my flat and have a hot shower!

Massini is something of an anomaly among the Christmas Eve queuers though, as he's a professional musician and a former King's choral scholar who has seen the service from the other side – as a performer. His favourite Nine Lessons and Carols memory comes from his very first year in the choir.

> It was the beginning of the service – the solo treble had sung 'Once in Royal' and then we had sung our choir verse. Then suddenly, as we processed under

the organ and the congregation joined in for the first time, I caught sight of my mum and dad. Neither of them had ever been to King's before, and seeing their faces I just burst into tears. It was the most fantastic gift I could ever give back to them after all they'd given me. I'll remember that moment, watching their faces light up during that third verse, forever.

But what is it that draws Massini and others to return, year after year, to see the Festival of Nine Lessons and Carols? For many it's the beauty of the service – the combination of music, words, light and architecture that comes together to create something awesome in the truest sense of the word. For others the motivation is more personal, reconnecting with memories of Christmases past, of family rituals and experiences. The service is a touchstone, a constant in a changing world that helps people feel anchored and connected with their own history.

Inevitably, with such significance and such popularity, comes scrutiny and criticism. Each year since the radio broadcasts began, both King's and the BBC have received sackfuls of letters and even phone calls offering praise, feedback, advice, opinion and outright anger. Composer Bob Chilcott remembers the annual surge of public comment from his time at King's between 1965 and 1968.

People really do write a lot of angry letters! When I was a choral scholar, Philip Ledger [the then director of music] used to bring in all the correspondence and we'd read it. Much of it was very funny. It's like a soap opera – people feel a real sense of ownership of the service, and get offended when it deviates from what they think it should be. And in a way they are right – the public really do own the service.

Very few of the letters survive, but the handful that have been preserved make for lively – and varied – reading. One listener opines:

The Christmas service last Christmas Eve was in my opinion, the poorest, musically, I have ever heard. I have discussed this matter with a wide number of friends and relations, and the consensus of opinion is that there is an increasing number of cacophonous compositions which pass as carols being included in the service.

Another adopts a telegraphic approach.

Dear Sir, The Festival of Nine Lessons & Carols: 1993, Annus Horribilis. How could you do such a thing? But for the fact that I had a recording of a service from a former year, my Christmas would have been totally ruined.

While yet another simply requests:

Could you speed up your organ playing? It's more like a dirge. And the speakers could be more human too.

But for every criticism the choir receives come many, many letters of support and encouragement.

> Sir, I felt I had to write to you and say how much I enjoyed the Festival of Nine Lessons and Carols...As I listened, I realised that everyone (like myself) spending Christmas alone could never really be alone when such a beautiful service could be brought right into our home. Would you thank everyone who took part in this special service and tell them the joy that they must have brought to so many people.

'Once in Royal'

Listeners over the years have taken issue with everything from the acoustic to the recording quality, from the organ playing to the choice of carols, but one aspect of the service that is almost universally beloved, that seems somehow inviolate, set apart from the rest of the ritual, is the opening verse of 'Once in Royal'.

Although originally sung by all the choristers, a tradition developed early on in the evolution of the Festival of Nine Lessons and Carols for the verse to go to a single solo treble. The fragility and beauty of that lone voice, its innocence and purity, is, for many, the essence of Christmas itself – a moment of stillness and truth in an ever-more chaotic world. There's something about a boy's voice that's particularly emotive. Typically aged 12 or 13, these solo choristers have maybe months left, a year if they're lucky, with their treble voices. What we hear in that perfect solo moment is an artist at the peak of their maturity, whose gift is on the cusp of disappearing forever. It's a powerful idea, and an even more powerful aesthetic experience.

Speaking to music historian Nicholas Nash, conductor Sir Neville Marriner (whose own son, Andrew, was a King's chorister) shared his experience of the peculiar alchemy of this musical moment.

Somehow from the moment the first boy starts to sing, there's a shiver that runs down your back. From that moment until the end of the Service and lingering long afterward, you have this extraordinary emotional upheaval which has the habit of recurring. You always think, 'this could never happen to me again.' And when you hear it again, exactly the same thing happens.[13]

Part of the magic, the mystique of that moment, is that nobody knows in advance which boy will be chosen to sing the solo – not even the boys themselves, or sometimes not even the director of music. In the lead-up to Christmas the director of music may coach four or five boys, and in the morning rehearsal for Nine Lessons and Carols he will give each of them an opportunity to sing the solo in full. But, come three o'clock that afternoon when the light on his monitor flashes solid red, he'll beckon just one boy forwards and the carol will begin.

But why this tense annual ritual? Isn't it all just hype? Jonathan Willcocks, son of long-time King's director of music David Willcocks, explains.

All choristers know who the strongest boys are, and who it is likely to be. In my generation Roy Goodman and Bob Chilcott both stood out. But it is also true that my father used not to actually tell the boys which chorister was going to sing it until the very last moment – largely so that their parents didn't get them all razzed up. If a chorister had known in advance then there was a danger that their family and friends might feed their nerves and wind them up, creating much more tension than the boy experiences in those few seconds between the director of music pointing at them and the moment they start to sing.

It may save on tension, but the process isn't without its own risks. History relates that, on at least one occasion, a director of music failed to indicate his choice sufficiently clearly, and two boys stepped forwards simultaneously.

Bob Chilcott, a regular 'Once in Royal' soloist during his time in the choir in the 1960s, remembers the process fondly.

David Willcocks was really wonderful – he'd work with you a great deal before the day itself, coaching you carefully until you were really confident. I remember standing there in the chapel ready to sing and him telling me, 'See all the rows of people out there? Just imagine that they are all cabbages.'

Gabriel May, a King's chorister from 2011–15 was also lucky enough to sing the solo – an experience he'll never forget.

It's pretty much every chorister's dream to sing 'Once in Royal', but we're all good mates in the choir so we weren't that competitive. I was lucky enough to get it and my friends were very nice about it. At the moment when the red light started flashing I just looked up to the back of the chapel and thought, 'This is amazing. This is my dream.' But I wasn't actually too nervous because there just wasn't time. I was mostly just excited. The whole experience was unbelievable. Every now and then I do listen back to it – it's a bit weird, seeing yourself on television or on YouTube.

The Arrival of Boris Ord

The experience each generation of choristers and choral scholars has in King's Chapel may not have changed much in over 100 years, but their lives in the college itself, at school and back in the boarding house have altered beyond recognition. The twentieth century saw some of the most dramatic changes – a shift from the Victorian regime of A.H. Mann to the contemporary practices of David Willcocks, evolving gradually through the transitional period of music director Boris Ord.

Bernhard Ord (known to all as Boris – a nickname apparently inspired by his love of Mussorgsky's opera *Boris Godunov*) succeeded Mann in 1929. He had already been appointed a fellow of King's in 1923, and in 1926 – at Mann's request – became assistant organist, helping ensure a smooth continuity between the by now very elderly Mann's regime and his own. If his musical tastes were more progressive than his predecessor's, extending to the newly fashionable Tudor composers, seventeenth-century verse anthems with viols, as well as contemporary works by Herbert Howells, John Ireland and Ralph Vaughan Williams, his standards were every bit as exacting and his methods every bit as old-fashioned in their rigour.

Patrick Magee, a chorister under Mann and later a choral scholar under Ord, remembers vividly the shift between the two eras.

> Boris's method didn't differ much from those of Mann, but his personality did. Having all the vigour of a much younger man he drove the choir more aggressively and could be bitingly sarcastic. We would come out of the chapel after a stormy session feeling rather small, when Boris would walk out calmly, have a drink in his rooms or in the pub and chat happily as though nothing but amiable thoughts had crossed his mind. In other words he treated us as professionals inside chapel, but once outside we were friends.
>
> Boris's contrasting attitudes inside and outside chapel were matched by his way of life. In his personal arrangements he was notoriously unpunctual and

HERBERT HOWELLS: 'A SPOTLESS ROSE'

Boris Ord was a great champion of twentieth-century British composers, including Herbert Howells, whose 'A Spotless Rose' remains a King's favourite today. Howells's text is a free translation of verses better known in German as 'Es ist ein Ros' entsprungen'. They describe Christ's birth as a flower blooming, not in spring, but in the 'cold winter' and the 'dark midnight'. Composed in 1919, that 'dark midnight' must have seemed hopeless indeed to the composer who lost close friends and colleagues in the war, spicing the hopeful innocence and certainty of this carol with a powerful pathos. The music itself seems oddly timeless – the melody has something of plainchant about it, free-flowing, growing organically just like the flower it describes. The carol closes with music so exquisite (setting the words 'cold winter's night') that composer Patrick Hadley declared he should like to pass away while listening to it.

chaotic in organisation. Piles of letters would accumulate on the seat inside his door, and periodically we were asked to help him sort them out....In contrast to this, arrangements for all chapel music were made with complete precision: all lists meticulously compiled. Practices started at 4.15pm. Boris would arrive at 4.14pm precisely, and if anyone was late we would all know about it. No one ever was.

In many ways, though, college life continued much as it had for centuries, with the student choral scholars still looked after as their predecessors had been by 'bedmakers' (a term shortened by today's students to 'bedders') – the college servants responsible for waking the young men in the morning, brushing their clothes and helping with any small chores. They were, however, as Magee recalls, anything but subservient, quite capable of putting their charges in their place.

We would be woken by the bedmaker in the morning, who in winter would also light the fire (the only form of heating at the time) and lay breakfast. These bedmakers were considerable characters who had strong opinions on how undergraduates should conduct themselves. 'I do like gen'lemen to be gen'lemen' observed Mrs X., but we failed to draw her further on her ideas of the species. However, on a later occasion she was holding forth on one of her past charges: 'Proper gen'leman he was – sick all down the stairs.' So then we knew.

Magee's contemporary at King's, both as a chorister and later a choral scholar, David Briggs, also remembers his student days at the college in that precarious prewar period of the 1930s with tremendous fondness.

When I was a choral scholar I was always very fond of games but found that choir practices always clashed with team ones so I could never join. I thought if I had a horse that it would be one way of getting some exercise. So I got permission from the college to keep my 17-hands horse, Tiny, in Scholars' Piece at the back of the college for a shilling a week. I kept a sort of miniature haystack in my rooms in Gibbs Building to feed him. One night at about 3am the porter knocked on my door and told me that Tiny had jumped over the fence and was eating the crocuses and could I please do something about it. So I had to go out in my pyjamas and fetch him back.

But despite the many distractions of college life, the quality of music at King's had never been higher. Ord was one of the first major directors of music, whether in an Oxbridge choral foundation or at a cathedral, to give greater priority to training the choir than to his own organ-playing duties, and the result was an ever-more carefully tuned and rhythmically precise ensemble. In an address to the Royal College of Organists, George Guest, director of music at St John's College, Cambridge, paid homage to Ord's influence and his considerable legacy.

In the late 1940s some of us in Cambridge used to watch Boris Ord rehearsing his choir with little less than awe. We admired his technique but, above all, were electrified by his personality – and it was his personality, of course, which inspired his choir. It was partly to do with his choice of words, partly to do with the particularly characteristic sound of his voice, partly to do with the precision and rhythmic vitality of his gestures, but, above all, to do with his eyes – it is in the eyes of a conductor that a member of the choir finds inspiration.[14]

Ord may not have been a prolific composer or arranger like later King's directors of music have tended to be, but his legacy to the choir does also include one carol that has become part of the furniture of the service of Nine Lessons and Carols. Ord's setting of this anonymous fifteenth-century text is his only published composition – a work whose forthright simplicity pays homage to the text's medieval colour without losing its identity as a contemporary work.

Adam lay ybounden,
Bounden in a bond;
Four thousand winter
Thought he not too long.
And all was for an apple,
An apple that he took,
As clerkës finden
Written in their book.
Nor had one apple taken been,
The apple taken been,
Then had never Our Lady
A-been heaven's queen.
Blessed be the time
That apple taken was.
Therefore we may singen
Deo gratias!

The text tells that oldest story of Adam's temptation and his fall, but puts a rather unusual spin on it. Yes, Adam was condemned to suffering as a result of his weakness, but if, reasons the author, the apple had not been taken, then the Virgin Mary would never have become Queen of Heaven. For this reason, he declares, we must rejoice with cries of 'Deo Gratias' ('Praise God'). Ord sets the text to a lilting waltz-like melody that anticipates the carol's joyful ending, even while its text speaks of darker matters. The closing 'Deo Gratias' has a glorious sense of release, breaking out of the carol's neat four-bar phrases for this final, extended shout of festive joy.

It adds a certain extra savour to this classic carol to know that King's very nearly missed out on it altogether. The original set of copies, handwritten by Ord himself, were lost just before the carol was first broadcast, and only the composer hastily rewriting them all from scratch saved the situation and preserved the carol.

Adam Lay Ybounden

A - dam lay y - boun - den, Boun - den in a bond:

Four thou - sand win - ter Thought he not too long.

King's Under Fire – the Second World War

But the joy of the interwar years at King's was to be fleeting, cut cruelly short by the outbreak of the Second World War in 1939. At first things continued as usual, an odd, uncanny atmosphere tainting the normal ritual of college life, but gradually students, fellows and servants all began to be called up, and RAF soldiers, billeted at the college, arrived in their stead. Trenches were dug outside the choir school, military vehicles lined the lawns down on to the Backs and, most strikingly, in 1941 the beautiful chapel windows were removed for safety and replaced with black tar paper.

The windows themselves, long thought to have been dispatched to Welsh slate mines for protection, were actually stored in numerous cellars across Cambridge, including the college's own. Their removal left the chapel itself all but open to the elements. The tar paper provided little by way of protection against bad weather and rattled horribly in the wind. With no heating to combat this, services became, for a time, something of an endurance test, and with few choral scholars remaining, sung services were reduced to weekends, continuing with the help of singing volunteers.

During this period, Ord, who like Milner-White had seen active service during the Great War, returned once again to the RAF, leaving King's Choir temporarily in the hands of Harold Darke. One of the great organists of his day, Darke was also responsible for composing a setting of one of the loveliest Christmas carols – 'In the Bleak Midwinter' – a carol voted the best of all time in a 2008 survey of choral conductors and directors undertaken by BBC *Music* magazine.

Composed when Darke was still a student at the Royal College of Music in 1909, this setting of Christina Rossetti's poem shows extraordinary musical maturity. The beauty of the verse is all in its simplicity, and to overload it with musical sentiment or complexity would be to lose its delicate landscape under a snowdrift.

GUSTAV HOLST: 'IN THE BLEAK MIDWINTER'

Harold Darke's setting may have beaten Gustav Holst's in the BBC *Music* magazine's 2008 poll, but this 1906 carol – commissioned by Vaughan Williams – is still beloved by listeners. Simpler than the Darke, it is a proper congregational hymn with none of the variation between verses that the later composer allows himself, the beauty of Holst's setting is its unexpected melancholy – there's a real sense of yearning, created by harmonies for whom resolution doesn't come easily. Like the Nativity story itself, a joyful ending is only achieved after suffering. Holst's melody goes by the name 'Cranham' – named after the Gloucestershire village where the composer wrote it.

The carol is strophic – written in repeating verses – but you'd scarcely know it, so varied are the moods and textures Darke conjures to colour each repetition. The fragility of the opening treble solo with rocking organ accompaniment gives way to a muscular second verse – 'Our God, Heaven cannot hold Him' – swapping human frailty for the strength of God. And then comes the coup de grâce. Rossetti's final verse pivots; suddenly the focus turns inwards – 'What can I give Him, / Poor as I am?' This shift to 'I' is matched by Darke in a musical gesture that strips away the supporting scaffolding of the bassline. Left alone, the treble and alto voices seem horribly exposed, inadequate almost. But as conviction grows in the text, so does the strength of the music, and we finish with an ecstatic embellishment – the trebles just kiss a high G on the word 'heart', a musical gesture charged with all the spontaneous generosity of the text.

Choristers in Wartime

The choral scholars may have missed the war years at Cambridge, but school life continued for the choristers – with a few less-than-pleasant changes. With so many domestic staff called up by the army, the boys were forced to step in to keep the school running, serving variously as kitchen porters, gardeners and cleaners. Apparently, during these years, the headmaster only had to shout 'Gang!' and a group of boys would immediately materialise and set to scrubbing floors or laying tables, as required. But even their best efforts couldn't quite maintain prewar standards, and some things were let slide – notably bedsheets, which were changed only twice a term. With dormitory windows sealed with blackout material, the smell must have been rather alarming by the time the holidays arrived.

But it wasn't all work. Headmaster Cedric Moulton Fiddian (known to all as Fid) was a keen, not to say obsessive, sportsman, and insisted all his charges share his enthusiasm. The minute the winter frost hit the Cam, lessons were abandoned for skating sessions on Grantchester Meadows. The pragmatic rule – unimaginable in today's health and safety-obsessed climate – was that skating continued until the first boy fell through the ice, at which point conditions were deemed unsafe. So cold was the winter of 1946–7, and so perfect the winter-sports conditions, that 'hardly a lesson took place' during the first six weeks of term.

The English Carol Revival

We've already seen just how much Eric Milner-White's service of Nine Lessons and Carols owes to its time. It spoke both to and – crucially – for a generation, and fed a shared need that nobody till then had fully recognised or articulated. Musically too, the service was very much a product of its day – not only bringing the Christmas carol, still a bespectacled, specialist sort of genre, into the musical mainstream, but also providing a new platform and focus for the work of a generation of outstanding British composers. It's no coincidence that so many of the twentieth-century English greats, from Ralph Vaughan Williams and Gustav Holst to Herbert Howells and Benjamin Britten, took a strong interest in choral music in general and in carols in particular.

So many of the carols we love and look forward to as part of King's Nine Lessons and Carols today come from these early decades of the service – the 1930s–50s. These works may not have quite the romance of their medieval ancestors, nor the sentimental directness of their Victorian grandparents, but they have a character and charm that's all their own. At a time of national and international uncertainty, while the maps of Europe and the colonial world were being dramatically redrawn, they cultivated a musical corner that was 'forever England'. With one foot in the musical past and the other in the present, they built a bridge back to lost traditions, reinventing Christmas and its mystery for a new generation. There's new sophistication in these carol-anthems, certainly, but there's also wonder and innocence, a memory of the folk songs and the medieval melodies in which this music has its roots.

After all the efforts of the Victorians, it's hard to believe that the English Christmas carol really was – once again – in need of a revival in the early twentieth century. It doesn't paint a great picture of the robust health of the genre, fainting away like some tubercular heroine as soon as popular attention was diverted elsewhere. In its defence though, it's not that the carol had died out altogether, more perhaps that it had taken a diversion on its journey, one that had led it away from the parlours and parishes of bustling cities and on to little-known rural tracks, frequented only by knapsack-wearing, notebook-clutching folk-music specialists.

The extent to which Christmas carols had been abandoned by the general public is made overwhelmingly clear in an article published in the December 1928 issue of the *Radio Times* – the same issue that advertised the very first broadcast of *Carols from King's*. Written by Henry Walford Davies (a future Master of the King's Music, and himself the composer of a popular alternative melody for 'O Little Town of Bethlehem'), the article laments with terrifying pomposity the decline of the carol and attempts some explanation for this oversight.

> Christmas hymns and melodies are legion, but only a
> few special favourites seem to be heard in churches today,
> and fewer still have found their way into the repertoire
> of carol-singers in the streets (notably, of course, 'While
> Shepherds Watched', sung until we are all temporarily

tired of its noble tune 'Winchester')...Why not? It
is rather to be feared that the pressure of Christmas
occupations, and a certain culpable inertia present in
many of us, combine to crowd out much loveliness and
to keep our repertoire severely down.

Moral righteousness aside, Walford-Davies does raise
two interesting questions: what caused this second dip
in the carol's popularity, and what was it that brought it
back to health and life? To answer we must pick up the
history of the carol where we left it, in the reverent hands
of Victorian collectors and editors Gilbert, Sandys and
their ilk (see page 81–2).

While religion and religious movements had fuelled the
surge in carols in Britain during the nineteenth century,
providing a hungry new market for all the anthologists
could deliver, in the twentieth century the carol revival was
driven by something altogether more secular: nationalism.
This involved first finding a way back to the pristine rural
idyll of the imagined past. Just look at Thomas Hardy's
novels and their fears for the disappearance of the simple,
superstitious England of *Tess of the D'Urbervilles* (1891) or *The
Woodlanders* (1887), lost under the rising tide of industrial
urban communities. The arrival of the machine and city
may have helped spread nineteenth-century Christmas
cheer, but it also contributed to the anxiety and creativity of
the twentieth century.

The response to such fears is clear to see. In 1898 the Folk Song Society was created, followed shortly in 1912 by the English Folk Dance Society, and in 1906 the Board of Education officially approved the teaching of folk songs in schools. These innovations speak of a nation keen not only to celebrate its history and identity, but also to mould and control it. Pioneering musical collectors such as Lucy Broadwood and Sabine Baring-Gould set off into the countryside armed with keen ears and freshly sharpened pencils to collect folk songs from locals, preparing the way for the work of Ralph Vaughan Williams, Cecil Sharp and Gustav Holst that would reach its climax in the influential *English Hymnal* (1906) and *The Oxford Book of Carols* (1928).

Hard though it is to believe now of a nation that counts Purcell, Elgar, Byrd, Britten and Parry among its musical heroes, as late as 1904 England was nicknamed 'Das Land ohne Musik' – the land without music. The nineteenth century was a bad time for England, musically speaking, with no composers to rival the Tchaikovskys, Griegs, Chopins and Wagners other nations could boast. So when Vaughan Williams and his colleagues were out collecting folk songs, and allowing those melodies and harmonies to seep into their own works, to colour them with the bittersweet, nostalgic pastoralism we now associate so strongly with English music, they weren't just preserving national tradition – they were inventing it.

Crucially, though, the tradition they were (re)inventing was not the sanitised and bowdlerised tradition of the Victorians, who dressed up folk carols in their Sunday best and sat them, hands nicely washed, in the parlour. Vaughan Williams was interested in a more masculine approach to carols, finding integrity and value in their rough corners and weatherworn musical facades, and no more wanting to prettify and embellish them than he would the ancient churches in which they were sung.

The Oxford Book of Carols

The Oxford Book of Carols (1928) was the manifesto for these new values – a little red book no less significant in its own sphere than Mao Tse-tung's more famous volume. Working with fellow editors Percy Dearmer and Martin Shaw, Vaughan Williams put together a collection of over 200 carols – not just traditional English ones, but foreign carols too, as well as newly composed works – that remains even today, nearly 40 editions later, the basis of our carol repertoire. Old tunes sometimes get new words, but remain otherwise faithful to their origins, lovingly traced in the historical notes that gloss each carol. Arrangements are delicate but never precious, sensitive to the origins of their melodies, and above all accessible – capable of being performed in the home as well as by choirs in church.

One especially lovely folk carol included in the volume is 'Tomorrow Shall be My Dancing Day'. Although perhaps best known today in John Gardner's punchy, rhythmic setting, the traditional tune is an exuberant delight – an earworm that will refuse to leave you for days. There aren't many carols in 3/4 time (like a waltz), and this one makes the most of a rhythm that's more skipping country dance than sedate salon affair. The verse melody runs guilelessly up and down a simple scale, but it's the chorus that really makes the carol come alive. The ancient Cornish text has repetition built into it, 'Sing, oh! my love, oh! my love, my love, my love,', and the music responds to this, also repeating its melody to create an echoing effect, as though the singer's voice is heard while the singer herself dances on ahead, further and further away. The result is playful and joyful – like a musical game of tag that invites the listener to chase after the singer.

While the melody was first recorded by William Sandys in the nineteenth century, the words probably date back some 700 years and present something of a challenge for us today. Unusually, the carol is written in the first person, as though the infant Jesus himself is talking. He speaks of his 'dancing day' – the day of his birth – when he will come to earth to see his Church ('my true love') and invite her to join him in his dance of life. It's a captivating image, and one echoed in that other favourite hymn 'Lord of the Dance'.

One of the 'modern' carols popularised by *The Oxford Book of Carols* that has become a favourite, not just of Christmas services at King's but across the country, is Peter

Cornelius's 'The Three Kings'. In a musical sleight of hand that catches you somewhere between heart and throat each time you hear it, Cornelius sets his own text and melody for solo baritone – 'Three kings from Persian lands afar / To Jordan follow the pointing star' – above the exquisite sixteenth-century Lutheran chorale 'Wie schön leuchtet der Morgenstern' ('How Brightly Shines the Morning Star'), sung by the choir. The pairing of Cornelius's innocent verse, originally designed to explain the story of the Three Wise Men to children, and the mystical, barely revealed beauty of the chorale text, adapted from Psalm 45, creates a wonderful sense of breadth, inviting us all to find our own place in this story.

The two texts are further connected, drawn together by the delicacy with which Cornelius manages to weave his own melody through the chorale. The regular tread

DID YOU KNOW?

The version of Peter Cornelius's 'The Three Kings' that we know today is vastly different from its first incarnation, as a solo song cycle for baritone and piano. And but for Liszt's timely intervention and suggestion, the carol wouldn't have included the chorale that makes the piece so magical.

The Three Kings

Three kings from Per - - sian lands a

How

- far To Jor - dan fol - low the point - ing star:

bright - ly shines the morn - ing star!

and even phrases of the chorale serve as the anchor for the soaring phrases of the soloist that dive and duck among them like a child, never settling or achieving resolution, too eager to arrive at the manger and worship the Christ Child to contain its excitement. It's a classic piece of songwriting – just swap the cassock-wearing soloist for Bing Crosby and the choir for a studio backing group, and you'd have all the ingredients for a huge Christmas hit.

Looking to Europe

But not all English composers were as drawn to folk music as Vaughan Williams and his fellow editors of *The Oxford Book of Carols*. Some preferred to celebrate England's musical heritage by looking back to medieval and Renaissance manuscript sources. Unlike folk songs, they argued, these works were authentic and absolute, not likely to be misremembered, altered or unconsciously edited down the centuries by their performers. Holst and Peter Warlock took inspiration from these early texts and melodies, but perhaps neither more fruitfully than the 16-year-old Benjamin Britten.

Confined to his boarding school sanatorium by illness, the teenage Britten wrote the carol that would arguably become his best-loved work – 'A Hymn to the Virgin'. It's a work that carries great significance on slight musical shoulders, gaining the composer entry to the Royal College of Music, and eventually becoming one of only two pieces performed at his funeral. 'A Hymn to the Virgin' is a perfect miniature, setting an anonymous medieval text with a delicacy that occasionally gets overshadowed in Britten's later works by complexity.

The composer divides his eight voices into two four-part choirs. While one remains grounded in all things earthly by its English text, and in the human by its emotional crescendos and climaxes, the other is set at a distance. Singing only in Latin, these other-worldly solo voices echo and transmute the utterances of the first choir into music that's unchanging, eternal. In Britten's hands a simple, strophic carol-hymn is itself transfigured.

Peter Warlock (a name, alas, too good to be true – actually the pseudonym for one Philip Heseltine) was another composer drawn to all things medieval. His own adopted name was a nod to his fascination with the occult, and his interests extended also to Renaissance art, the Tudor composers, as well as other rather more scurrilous (but no less historical) pastimes. Both his 'Corpus Christi Carol' and 'Balulalow' blend the composer's own bittersweet harmonic voice with medieval texts, artfully smudging the illuminated-manuscript clarity of their images with his watercolour choral textures. But Warlock's unquestioned carol masterpiece, 'Bethlehem Down', the one work you have to know (and one you only have to know in order to love), takes inspiration from rather less lofty sources.

Here He has peace and a short while for dreaming,
Close huddled oxen to keep Him from cold,
Mary for love, and for lullaby music
Songs of a shepherd by Bethlehem fold.

It is one of those melodies that, even at first hearing, you'd swear you've known forever. But despite its graceful, arching lines and the tender sadness of its harmonies, the carol was the product of a deeply pragmatic need for cash on the part of two penurious artists hoping to fund their Christmas booze-up. Journalist Bruce Blunt, author of the carol's lyrics, explains:

> In December 1927, we were both extremely hard up, and, in the hope of being able to get suitably drunk at Christmas, conceived the idea of collaborating on another carol which should be published in a daily paper. So, walking on a moonlit night between the Plough at Bishop's Sutton and the Anchor at Ropley, I thought of the words of 'Bethlehem Down'. I sent

them off to Philip in London, the carol was completed in a few days and published (words and music) in *The Daily Telegraph* on Christmas Eve. We had an immortal carouse on the proceeds and decided to call ourselves 'Carols Consolidated'.[15]

But, listening to the carol – to its supple verse, which distils the Christian story down to a series of startlingly simple images, and to music that speaks hopefully of love and peace even while in the distance we see the silhouette of Calvary – it's impossible to hear any cynicism or pragmatism, just beauty.

Sitting precisely at the junction of Church and pub, somewhere between piety and an anarchic good time, 'Bethlehem Down' is the essence of the twentieth-century carol – the natural child of the medieval carol and the Victorian carol, a perfect distillation of a long history into a living form.

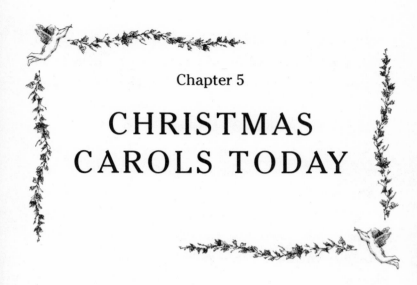

Chapter 5

CHRISTMAS CAROLS TODAY

What sweeter music can we bring
Than a carol, for to sing
The birth of this our heavenly King?
Awake the voice! Awake the string!

(Robert Herrick, 1591–1674)

Christmas carols are traditionally the very sweetest of music: tender cradle songs and lullabies, joyful dances and musical shouts of celebration. The Victorians made Christmas in their own image, stuffed to overflowing with sugar and spice and a generous glug of sentimentality. It's a taste that's cloying to the contemporary palate, but one we still cling to, craving the comfort and beauty of a bygone age.

But what of our own age? If 'Hark! The Herald' and 'Away in a Manger' are the soundtrack to Victorian piety and nostalgic innocence, then what is the music that speaks of a world that's suddenly so much louder, brighter and harsher? And where do we find these contemporary carols – in churches and chapels, or in concert stadiums and cinemas, on the radio and television?

The answer, perhaps, is all of the above. Christmas carols that started their lives so many centuries ago in streets and homes have reached a fork in the road. Some have continued on the familiar path that leads to the door of King's College Chapel, while others have turned back, ripping off their chorister's ruffs and robes and sloping off to the pub, choosing instead to return to the carol's domestic roots – a popular song, whistled while washing-up, walking home or belted out karaoke-style at the office Christmas party.

But if carols really are 'songs…that are simple, hilarious, popular, and modern', as no less an authority than *The Oxford Book of Carols* claims, then it's easy to see that Slade's 'Merry Xmas Everybody', The Pogues and Kirsty MacColl's 'Fairytale of New York' and even Wham!'s 'Last Christmas' have as good, if not an even better, claim on the genre than the nostalgic fantasy of 'It Came Upon a Midnight Clear' or the artful artlessness of Christmas anthems by Benjamin Britten or John Tavener. Yet carols have long had one foot in church and another in the mead hall, and the twenty-first-century carol's dramatic split down the middle is, in many ways, a continuation and sustaining of tradition rather than a break with it.

The Man Who Transformed Christmas Carols

But before we earn our trip to the pub to shout our way through 'Do They Know it's Christmas?', we must first return to King's Chapel. Boris Ord, like A.H. Mann before him, continued as organist and director of music at King's until his death. In 1958, David Willcocks – himself a former King's organ scholar – was officially named his successor. It's no exaggeration to say that it was an appointment that transformed not only Christmas at King's, but Christmas across the Western world, reinvigorating the carol and amplifying it with innovations so instinctive and inevitable that, like Christmas trees and cards before them, we struggle to remember a time before they existed.

Those who worked with Willcocks, whether at King's or later at the Royal College of Music, remember a man charged with energy. Willcocks served in the army during the Second World War, working behind enemy lines as an intelligence officer and later gaining the Military Cross for leading his heavily depleted battalion to victory after the death of their commanding officer. His leadership was instinctive, whether in battle or with his young choristers, fuelled not by ambition but by a profound interest in people, a sympathy and understanding that recurs again and again in the descriptions of those who knew him.

Opera singer Richard Suart, a chorister under Willcocks in the early 1960s, recalls, 'A wonderful and very friendly man, interested not just in me but in my entire family, someone extraordinarily gifted with people.' Willcocks's people skills, combined with an intuitive musical ability, an unwavering insistence on excellence and a healthy streak of fun (his party trick was to play the piano with his back to it, hands crossed over his shoulders, and, when a castaway on *Desert Island Discs* in 1998, he cheekily requested no less than King's College Chapel as his luxury), Willcocks was the force that took King's to new heights.

Competitive in the best possible way, jealous to ensure the very best choral and organ scholars applied not to St John's or other Cambridge rivals but to King's, Willcocks was not above indulging in some gentle showmanship to make his case, as composer John Rutter recalls.

> King's Chapel has quite a staggering effect on people. If any talented organ scholar candidate had the temerity to put any other college as first choice on his application, David would always invite them in to the chapel to see him just as the sun was setting through the west window. He'd ensure that the choir was singing something stirring like Parry's 'I was glad'. Later, he'd remark: 'If that doesn't get him, nothing will!'

The choir that Willcocks inherited from Ord was one of professional quality, drilled to deliver only the most blended of tone (woe betide any chorister or choral scholar whose voice blurted out above the rest) and the most exact tuning. But it was under Willcocks that King's College Choir became the ensemble we recognise today from recordings and broadcasts, a model not only of purity and precision, but also of expressive sensitivity and vocal drama.

But shaping the sound of the choir was only part of Willcocks's legacy to King's. His greatest contribution was music itself – the many carol arrangements and descants he created for the choir are musical grafts that have taken so completely that you can no longer see where the original ends and the addition begins. For people of my generation, Christmas sounds as Willcocks imagined it to sound; we've never known it any other way. To hear 'O Come All Ye Faithful' without the joyous, trumpet-like fanfare that is his 'Sing, choirs of angels' melody for the trebles, rising boldly above the congregation in the penultimate verse, is to hear it incomplete, unfinished. To hear an alternative descant (and there are now plenty) is just never quite right – like eating a Christmas cake made to someone else's family recipe.

It all started in 1958, in the run-up to Willcocks's very first Festival of Nine Lessons and Carols as director of music, as the conductor himself recalls in William Owen's *A Life In Music* (2008).

I thought how dull it is always to have the hymns just sung in unison. I thought I would like to add one or two new descants and arrangements...A lot of people afterwards wrote to say how much they had enjoyed the descants. Well, somebody from Oxford University Press heard these and asked if they could have the three carols. I had never had anything published before, but I thought, 'Let them have it.'[1]

As it turned out, that casual agreement was the beginning of something much bigger – a 30-year relationship with Oxford University Press that would produce the iconic Carols for Choirs series, the beloved 'green book (1961)', the 'orange book' (1970) and their 1978, 1980 and 2011 sequels that would change the carol landscape from 'Here be dragons' barrenness to ubiquitous familiarity. Even today, nearly 50 years on, there's almost no one in the English-speaking world who sings, whether in a school choir, at church, in a chamber choir or choral society, who couldn't whistle Willcocks's lilting organ accompaniment for the 'Sussex Carol' or hum his pealing bell-song reworking of 'Ding Dong Merrily on High'. Harmonies and musical textures we take for granted, whether they're for 'Angels from the Realms of Glory', 'Deck the Halls' or 'See Amid the Winter's Snow', weren't the result of gradual evolution, of generations of musical Chinese whispers by church organists; they were composed by the imaginative and impossibly skilled trio of Willcocks and his collaborators Reginald Jacques and John Rutter.

Today we're spoilt for choice when it comes to carol arrangements, available in creative editions for everything from nursery-school children to recorder ensembles and kazoo orchestras. But this is a recent phenomenon. In 1960, if you wanted to put together a carol service for your amateur choir (especially if you didn't happen to have an accompanist or, at the other end of the spectrum, if you preferred to use an orchestra) you'd struggle to find convenient resources beyond the now rather elderly *Oxford Book of Carols*. Not only did Willcocks and his *Carols For Choirs* collaborator Reginald Jacques fill a gap in the market, they all but created the genre of the choral-society carol concert – loosening the professionals' grip on carols and making them once again accessible to all, as well as providing a welcome alternative to the endless *Messiah*s that were then a weary fixture of Christmas.

Composer John Rutter, who would go on to collaborate with Willcocks on the series after the death of Jacques, recalls his momentous first encounter with the 'green book'.

> I was still in short trousers when it came out in 1961, but I remember quite clearly the occasion I first heard anything from it, because John Tavener brought it along to choir practice at the church in Kensington where he was organist as a teenager. He opened it at 'O Come All Ye Faithful' and played us Willcocks's

'Sing, choirs' descant. We clustered around the organ, all gobsmacked at how it just lights up the musical sky.

With a lot of the best ideas you find yourself saying, 'Why did no one think of that before?' To borrow the 'Gloria' refrain of 'Ding Dong Merrily' and use it as a descant is such a simple but bold thing to have done – it brings together two well-loved melodies in one carol without sounding at all contrived.

What makes this particular descant all the more startling is that it was written not laboriously or formally, but scribbled down while on a train late one Monday evening – a passing moment of inspiration as Willcocks made his way back to Cambridge after conducting a Bach Choir rehearsal in London.

Ding Dong Merrily on High

1. Ding dong! mer-ri-ly on high in heav'n the bells are ring-ing:
2. E'en so here below, be-low, let stee-ple bells be swung-en,
3. Pray you, du-ti-ful-ly prime your Ma-tin chime, ye ring-ers;

Ding dong! ver-i-ly the sky is riv'n with An-gel sing-ing.
And i - o, i-o, i - o, by priest and peo-ple sung-en.
May you beau-ti-ful-ly rime your Eve-time Song, ye sing-ers:

Glo - - - - - - - -

- - - - ri-a, Ho-san-na in ex-cel-sis!

WHAT IS A DESCANT?

At its simplest, a descant is just a melody. It's a melody sung by the highest voices in a choir, designed to fit with a carol or hymn tune like a piece of musical jigsaw puzzle. The descant sits above the original melody, complementing and embellishing it. Almost unknown before the twentieth century, in the hands of skilled composers such as Vaughan Williams and David Willcocks, the descant has gone on to become a much-loved fixture of hymns and Christmas carols, bringing them to a spectacular climax when added to the last verse.

First Television Broadcast

Although the choir's very first televised service of Nine Lessons and Carols took place in 1954 under Boris Ord, it wasn't until Willcocks's day that this broadcast became a regular fixture, joining the much-loved radio transmission as an essential part of Christmas. For the first time people could not only hear the celebrated choir, but also see the breathtaking beauty of King's Chapel itself. It's the images from these early broadcasts – small boys in robes singing in candlelit choir stalls – that caught hold of the public imagination so tightly, and still show no signs of letting go.

The paper trail at the BBC leading up to these first experiments with television is a fascinating one. As early as 1952 we find an internal memo by staffer Patricia Foy (who would go on to become a celebrated director and producer) tentatively mooting the idea.

> I am certain the idea of televising the Festival of Nine Lessons and Carols from King's College, Cambridge on Christmas Eve has already been considered, but if not, please may I suggest that this might make an acceptable transmission?[2]

It was clearly a suggestion that stuck, but one that also raised sufficient difficulties for George Barnes, director of television broadcasting, to describe it in a 1954 letter to King's provost Stephen Glanville as 'what is, I believe, a vexing question for the College'.[3] The same letter makes intriguing reference to a much earlier attempt at televising the service from King's as part of the Festival of Britain in 1951, which had been aborted as a 'fiasco'. The challenges of the undertaking were enormous, and the almost decade-long gap between the first television broadcast of the Christmas Eve service in 1954 and the next attempt in 1963 perhaps owes more to the technical demands of the process than any artistic decision-making on the part of the BBC.

Jonathan Willcocks, David's son and a chorister at King's in the early 1960s, recalls the television broadcasts vividly.

> The television equipment was enormous – huge great mechanical things on trolleys. If they wanted a close-up of the choir they literally wheeled the camera right up in front of your face. And the lighting had to be hugely bright; there were these giant arc lamps everywhere, but of course we also had to have the candles lit to get that traditional feel to the chapel.

While the annual radio broadcast has always been a live affair, eavesdropping as unobtrusively as possible on the King's service of Nine Lessons and Carols, the television broadcast, which has gone out annually since the early 1990s, is something rather different – a cousin rather than a twin of its radio counterpart. Recorded in advance, usually a few weeks before Christmas, the television service is a specially created affair designed to translate the essence of the event for audiences at home, as BBC producer James Whitbourn explains.

> While the television broadcast is deeply rooted in the format of the original service of 1918, unlike the radio broadcast there isn't the same obligation to retain every element. For example, while the radio readings remain constant each year, the readings for television change and include non-biblical passages as well as biblical ones. Sometimes there's a theme – maybe he Virgin Mary or the Three Kings – and one year we commissioned a completely new set of readings from scratch. It's a chance to change the focus of the service, to create a poetic response to the biblical narrative offered by the radio broadcast.

Technically it's still a massive undertaking. The crew arrive at least three days before the recording to begin the painstaking and fiddly work of installing around thirty microphones in the ceiling and squeezing cameras everywhere from choir stalls to organ loft. King's Chapel is anything but easy to film in, it requires skilful camerawork. Beautiful though it is, the building is simply the wrong shape for television – tall and rectangular rather than low and square.

Another significant difference between the broadcasts – one that many people are either unaware of or prefer to ignore – is the famous 'Once in Royal' solo. Whitbourn says:

> It's misleading to think that the solo chorister for the television broadcast is chosen in the same way as for radio. Actually what happens is that we record four or five choristers in advance and then make a choice afterwards. In that respect it doesn't have quite the romance that people like to imagine – it's done very professionally and the boys take it all in their stride.

A Chorister's Christmas

But peering behind the curtain of the perfect King's Christmas Eve service doesn't always mean spoiling the illusion. We might see and hear the 16 choristers of the choir at their most formal and professional in the Festival of Nine Lessons and Carols – each with a perfectly knotted tie and immaculately brushed hair, singing with absolute unanimity and precision – but behind the scenes today's choristers still enjoy the same riotous Christmas fun as their predecessors.

The 'Slack' – the period between the end of the school term and the end of the choir's singing duties on Christmas Day – remains a favourite time of year.

With only the choristers left in the boarding house, rules are relaxed and normal timetables replaced by a busy schedule of outings and events – trips to the pantomime and concerts, cracker-making and cooking, presents and parties – all fitted in between rehearsals. Gabriel May, a chorister from 2011–15, remembers it with enthusiasm.

> The teachers all try and make the boarding house as homely as possible. Leading up to Christmas there's always a dorm decorating competition – we make our own decorations and paper chains and put them up ourselves. And on Christmas Eve, after the long services, all our families come together for a Christmas Eve meal.

Even the staff get into the spirit of things. Gerald Peacocke, headmaster of King's College School from 1977–93, recalled his rather unusual duties each Christmas morning, which involved distributing the choristers' stockings. A simple enough task, surely? Not when the boys were allowed to prepare booby traps (wet, never dry) which he would have to overcome in order to gain access to their dormitories and deliver his bounty. The climax of the process would be an all-out assault by the boys, who would attack him enthusiastically with pillows until he shouted 'Pax!'

The King's Commissions

If David Willcocks's time at King's was defined by his carol arrangements, his instinctive ability to take an existing musical shell and fill it with new life and colour, then the current musical director Stephen Cleobury's tenure is characterised by brand-new carols. The conductor has described the King's carol tradition as a 'great oak tree', a tree that must continue to sprout new leaves if it is to survive. With that in mind, on his arrival in 1982, Cleobury immediately instigated his own tradition: each year the college would commission a new

HIGHLIGHTS OF THE KING'S COMMISSIONS

King's have commissioned a new carol for their Christmas Eve service for over 30 years, generating a huge catalogue of music. So where do you start?

Lovers of melody can't do better than Rutter's 'Dormi Jesu' or Gabriel Jackson's 'The Christ Child', both serenely beautiful lullaby-inspired settings.

Musical storytelling is at the fore in Jonathan Dove's 'The Three Kings' and Bob Chilcott's 'Shepherd's Carol', drawing listeners into the Christmas story, while dance rhythms animate the dark waltz of Carl Rutti's 'De Virgine Maria' and the helter-skelter joy of Arvo Pärt's 'Bogoróditse Djévo'.

carol from a significant composer, sustaining and feeding the Festival of Nine Lessons and Carols with the very best of contemporary choral music.

The results have been fascinating. The list of composers from 1983 to the present day is a roll call of great names, including the likes of Peter Maxwell Davies, John Tavener, John Rutter, Harrison Birtwistle, Jonathan Harvey, James MacMillan, Thomas Adès and Arvo Pärt. Many are composers not primarily associated with choral music, chosen deliberately by Cleobury in an attempt to integrate the often ghettoised world of Church composition more closely into the classical mainstream.

Contemporary Carols?

But this choice of composers raises an interesting question. How do we reconcile the complex, sophisticated anthems they produce with the carols we all know and love – simple, repetitive works with catchy choruses and melodies that you find yourself humming in the shower? At a glance, it's all but impossible to see the kinship between Giles Swayne's exquisite but inscrutable 'Winter Solstice Carol' (commissioned by King's in 1998), with its virtuoso solo flute-writing and fragmented, exploratory structure, and the homespun directness of 'While Shepherds Watched' or 'Away In a Manger'. So are these new works really carols at all?

John Rutter, one of only three composers to have been commissioned more than once for the King's Festival of Nine Lessons and Carols, argues that they are – almost.

> Of course the term 'carol' has had to be stretched to include what we should really call 'Christmas motets'. The difference is that while a motet is any piece for choir that happens to have a seasonal text, a carol – I think – implies something a bit more specific. You expect it to have verses and a refrain, and possibly also to be in some sense tuneful. You don't necessarily have to be able to walk out of the chapel whistling it, but I do feel it should make a nod in that direction. Judith Weir's 'Illuminare, Jerusalem' is a good example – it's almost in verses, and does have a refrain which comes round three times. But for me, a carol should always relate in some way to song, dance or lullaby – the three forms that you particularly associate with what 'carol' originally meant if you go back to the Middle Ages.

Rutter himself is the king of the twenty-first-century Christmas carol. You can't turn on BBC Radio 3 or Classic FM during December without hearing one of his choral works – musical miniatures whose sincerity speaks so directly to listeners. In a climate of growing suspicion towards contemporary classical music, Rutter is one of the few composers whose works have transcended genre and become genuinely popular – beloved for their memorable melodies and heartfelt response to text. But how does the composer himself explain his success?

> In many ways I'm probably more songwriter than composer. You'd have no expectation now, in 2016, that a concert composer would write a tune you could whistle, but you do still expect a songwriter to do that, and I think that's important. The great thing about a tune is that it's a wonderful carrier, a vector for the sense of a text. A good tune can carry a text right into the heart of a listener.

> The best advice I've ever been given was by my school composition teacher. He said: 'Write the music that's in your heart.' And that's what I've done.

Rutter's first commission from King's came in 1987, and the result – 'What Sweeter Music' – is a true modern classic, one of those rare moments of alchemy when text meets melody. Americans may recognise the tune as the sometime soundtrack to a Volvo advertisement, but should try not to hold that against it. The carol is a setting of seventeenth-century poet and cleric Robert Herrick's 'A Christmas Carol, Sung to the King in the Presence at White-Hall' – a clumsy title that in no way reflects the artless beauty of the verse. Herrick's conceit is simple; the birth of Christ transforms December to May, turning winter chill to spring life, filling meadows with corn and hearts with hope. Matching the simple joy of Herrick's verse is an endless arabesque of a melody, guided and held in the softest of harmonic embraces by its accompaniment.

While Rutter confesses that 'What Sweeter Music' was a work that came easily, flowing instinctively from his intimate knowledge of the choir, organ and chapel acoustic, others have struggled with the pressure of a King's commission and the scrutiny it brings. Bob Chilcott, himself an ex-King's chorister, is frank about his insecurities leading up to the premiere of his 'The Shepherd's Carol' in 2000.

> The idea of writing for that choir, as someone who had been in it, was just overwhelming. I spent a lot of time thinking that I'd never write a good enough piece; even when I got to the service itself I was convinced that they'd leave my piece out!

Chilcott's doubts were unfounded. His carol has become a recurring fixture of Nine Lessons and Carols – a piece Rutter has hailed as 'the most beautiful modern carol there is'. It's also the carol named by many of the current choristers and choral scholars as their favourite, beloved for its folk simplicity and a melody that feels as though it has always existed, unheard.

The carol's text – a heartfelt address from the shepherds to the Virgin – lends itself to Chilcott's unfussy treatment, giving a convincing musical voice not to sophisticated kings or heavenly angels but to simple shepherds: 'And so we have come, Lady, / Our day's work done, / Our love, our hopes, ourselves, / We give to your son.' The text itself, however, remains something of a mystery, as Chilcott explains.

> The theme for the television service that year was the shepherds, and the dean sent me over some possible texts, including this one. It must be a modern poem, but no person has ever come forward as the author. It has always been anonymous, and remains so.

The King's Commissions

Few contemporary British composers have captured the public imagination quite like John Tavener – a musician whose mystical gaze may have been fixed on a world beyond, but whose feet were firmly planted in the here and now. Over the course of an almost 50-year career, Tavener worked with Björk and the Beatles as well as with nuns and priests, produced Mercury Prize-nominated works as well as an eight-hour vigil and spoke as enthusiastically about cars as of the intricacies of religious rites. Tavener's large-scale works – his youthful cantata *The Whale* and his cello concerto *The Protecting Veil* – may have grabbed headlines, but it was his choral miniatures –his 'Song for Athene', sung so movingly at the funeral of Diana, Princess of Wales in 1997, and of course his carol 'The Lamb' – that transformed public admiration into affection.

Composed 'from seven notes in an afternoon', this setting of William Blake's poem from *Songs of Innocence and Experience* (1794) is an exercise in simplicity, distilling music down to the same allusive, charged essence as the poet's verse: 'Little lamb who made thee / Dost thou know who made thee'. Although not originally commissioned by King's (Tavener's 'Away In a Manger' was the commission for 2005), it's this carol that has become the composer's most frequent contribution to the Nine Lessons and Carols service, one of the most-recorded and most-performed carols of its age. When asked why listeners are so drawn to Tavener's spiritual music when we live in a secular age, Mother Thekla, the composer's long-time collaborator and spiritual muse, gave a simple answer: 'It reminds them of a time when they did believe in something'. It's impossible to hear this immaculate carol, glowing with simple beauty, and not feel stirred, to understand, as Eric Milner-White did, the role music and poetry play in faith.

'Bogoróditse Djévo'

While many of the King's commissions come from British composers, the college has also looked abroad to international figures such as Australia's Peter Sculthorpe ('The Birthday of Thy King', 1988), Finland's Einojuhani Rautavaara ('Christmas Carol', 2010) and America's Stephen Paulus ('Pilgrim Jesus', 1996) for their new carols. One of the most successful of these international commissions came from the Estonian composer Arvo Pärt.

In contrast to the meditative stillness and lullaby quality of the carols by Rutter, Chilcott and Tavener, Pärt's is a strikingly energetic affair, an unusually lively setting of 'Bogoróditse Djévo' – the Russian text of the Ave Maria – from a composer best known for the austere simplicity of his 'holy minimalism'. Barely a minute in length, the carol leaps into motion with a dancing motif in the upper voices – as though the singers are so overwhelmed with the joy of their text that they simply have to share it with their colleagues. But while the rhythm and the speed is all excitement, the hushed dynamic gives a wonderful sense of suppressed energy, of a (failed) attempt at self-control. Harmonically the carol is a perfect marriage of the Western choral tradition and the soundworld of Pärt's own Eastern Orthodox Church – a little bit King's and a little bit Constantinople.

'The Gleam'

But not all Cleobury's newly commissioned carols have received the same warm welcome as those of Chilcott, Tavener or Pärt. Every year since it started in 1928, the King's broadcast has provoked handfuls of letters from listeners to King's and to the BBC. The sound quality of the recording, the balance between organ and choir, and the quality of the choir itself all come in for regular comment, but by far the largest proportion of letters now focus on the new carols. Some are positive, others vehemently, emphatically the reverse. Talking to the *Guardian* in 2012, Cleobury recalled one such, which simply read: 'Whoever commissioned that carol should be locked in a darkened room and never let out.'[4] The carol in question? 'The Gleam' by that greatest of Britain's classical contrarians, Harrison Birtwistle.

Birtwistle, along with fellow composers Peter Maxwell Davies and Alexander Goehr, was one of a group of angry young men who first made their name at the Royal Manchester College of Music in the 1950s. Their anti-establishment rage may have been commonplace, but their talent was anything but, and their music has gone on to shape the landscape of contemporary British music.

'The Gleam' is typical of Birtwistle's jagged-edged genius. Making absolutely no concession to popular expectations of what a 'carol' might be, or to the traditionalists who would hold King's Nine Lessons and Carols in a permanent state of nostalgic suspension, the work is an extraordinary, confronting piece of musical atmosphere painting.

A curdled lullaby sets the scene, treating poet Stephen Plaice's refrain 'lalula, lalula / lalulaluel' more as primitive wail than soothing song. The infant Jesus sleeps in a dark, uncertain landscape where nothing is clear – veiled in the hazy, noncommittal choral chords that shift restlessly. As yet there are no shepherds, no Wise Men, no angels to rejoice, just a painful, private birth. But suddenly a 'six-pointed star' pierces the darkness, 'into her eye / enters the gleam.'. After such snow-muffled harmonies and gentle darkness the painful brilliance of the 'gleam' chord – white, bright, agonising – is heart-stopping. For some it's elbows-on-the-piano stuff, reason enough to condemn composer and commissioner alike to a locked room. But resist this knee-jerk horror and you'll find a carol that's the natural descendant of 'The Coventry Carol', 'Down in Yon Forest' or 'Adam Lay Ybounden', one that sees through the tinselly trappings of Christmas rejoicing to the human suffering beneath.

'The Flight'

Which brings us to the difficult question of relevance. In a world where our televisions pump out stories of war, famine and displaced peoples, where cruelty and violence are everywhere, do we look to Christmas and its carols as a nostalgic escape – a moment of determined hope and beauty in a troubled year – or do we seek something else from them, something that speaks to the doubts and darkness of our time? For composer Richard Causton, author of 'The Flight', 2015's commissioned carol, the choice was a simple one.

Searching for a text over the summer he found lots of beautiful fifteenth- and sixteenth-century poems, but nothing that could quite draw his attention away from the refugee crisis that dominated the news. To ignore the resonances of the Nativity and the flight into Egypt at such a time seemed almost perverse, and so he sought out a rather different kind of text.

> In the end I decided to ask the poet George Szirtes to write me something new. He was actually in Hungary when I called. It was the day when thousands of refugees were stranded at Budapest's Keleti railway station, and he'd actually been down there and spoken to them. He wrote the poem within 24 hours of seeing that. So yes, 'The Flight' feels different to many of the other King's commissions, but someone said to me after the service that there was a sense of relief that it spoke to current concerns. I don't understand why it doesn't occur to more people to connect these ideas – it feels very natural to me.

It was also a natural connection for Szirtes, a Hungarian whose own childhood was blighted by conflict. As an eight-year-old, Szirtes himself fled with his family, walking over the border into Austria during one long night in 1956.

'The Flight' is unapologetically contemporary. Ambulances and policemen bring the biblical tale of a perilous journey, a quest for the hope offered by the Christ Child, right up to date. But the carol also looks back, framing its images in rhyming couplets whose regularity, inevitability, seems to lull and comfort. A refrain – an exquisitely tender passage of music, standing apart from the babel of urgent voices that surrounds it – returns through the poem, a tender prayer for salvation: 'May those who travel light / Find shelter on the flight / May Bethlehem / Give rest to them.'. The sentiment here may be reassuring, but as the roaming harmonies of Causton's setting grasp after resolution, stretching and pulling ever further away from their starting point, we begin to question its easy response. Is prayer really enough when faced with such suffering? It's a question that haunts the mind, just as Causton's refrain echoes in the ears, long after listening to this poignant and angry work – a true contemporary carol, as the composer himself intended.

> I really wanted to write a *carol* – not a Christmas motet or an anthem. The repetitions and the refrain are crucial aspects of that – patterns that people can partake in and feel in a communal way. I don't have

illusions that the congregation would join in with my carol, but I do hope that the way the material comes round again and again will make it easier to grasp. Given the gravity of the subject matter, that is particularly important; I wanted it to lodge in people's minds.

Pop Songs or Christmas Carols?

When it comes to carols that lodge in people's minds, to tunes that barge into your ears and set up camp for the whole of December, the pop charts have the formula all worked out. Of course there's mistletoe and wine, sleigh bells jingling and chestnuts roasting, but there's also a streak of social conscience that manifests nowhere quite as clearly as Simon and Garfunkel's 1966 song '7 O'Clock News/Silent Night'. This chilling reimagining of the classic carol juxtaposes the duo singing the traditional melody in a softly cushioned two-part harmony with a spoken news report. As the track progresses, the report – with its accounts of a drug overdose, a civil-rights march and the horrific murder of a houseful of student nurses by Richard Speck – grows in volume while the singing fades away. The symbolism is all the more potent for its unignorable clarity: what use are the comforting carols of old in a world of such horrors?

'Do They Know it's Christmas?'

Taking a rather different approach to championing a social agenda is Band Aid's 'Do They Know it's Christmas?'. If this 1984 hit lacks the 'religious impulse' Percy Dearmer, editor of *The Oxford Book of Carols*, demanded of a true carol, it certainly fulfils all his other stipulations, being simple, popular and modern. Even the song's rather long-winded structure comes in (rather surprisingly) for Dearmer's approval: '[Carols] are generally spontaneous and direct in expression,' he writes, 'and their simplicity of form causes them sometimes to ramble on like a ballad.'

Shocked by reports of the Ethiopian famine that filled the news in 1984, Bob Geldof and Ultravox's Midge Ure decided to release a Christmas charity record to help. The only problem was that it was already November, allowing them none of the usual time for writing, recording and producing. Undeterred they persisted, coming up with the song themselves – cobbled together (in time-honoured carol tradition) from scraps of pre-existing material and a brand-new Christmassy melody by Ure – and gathering together the starriest supergroup imaginable, including George Michael, Boy George, Bono, Phil Collins and Sting. In just one day they laid down the track that would go on to become the UK's biggest-selling single of all time, a record it held for well over a decade.

The music press might have been sniffy, referring to the group as 'Bland Aid' and dismissing the song as an anticlimax after so much hype, but Geldof and Ure had the last laugh, raising over eight million pounds within a year of the song's release. They also started a Christmas tradition of their own. New recordings of the song in 1989, 2004 and 2014 would continue the original's charitable success. It's easy to trace a lineage from a carol like 'Good King Wenceslas' – not actively religious, but celebrating Christian kindness and charity – to 'Do They Know it's Christmas?', and even Causton's 'The Flight' belongs to this same family of carols. But where Band Aid's single differs is in intent. As Ure confesses in his autobiography, 'It is a song that has nothing to do with music. It was all about generating money. The song didn't matter: the song was secondary, almost irrelevant.'[5]

'Jingle Bells'

Commercial concerns are still a relatively new phenomenon when it comes to carols. Traditionally carols evolved, they weren't composed, they were owned by whoever was singing them in the moment. But with the rise of radio, cinema and television, carols became big business, changing to suit the taste of a market that preferred rosy-cheeked children and red-nosed reindeer to saints and angels.

OLD CAROLS, NEW LIVES

Carols continue to evolve, even today, thanks to the invention and creativity of pop and jazz artists. But which are the covers worth exploring?

- Jeff Buckley's stripped-back recording of the 'Corpus Christi Carol' is hauntingly lovely and deeply personal.

- 'Once in Royal' is transformed into a lilting country song in the hands of Mary Chapin Carpenter.

- No choir could bring the same poised solemnity to 'We Three Kings' that Ella Fitzgerald somehow achieves.

- Who knew Peter Warlock's 'Bethlehem Down' was hiding a slinky jazz number under its robes? The David Rees-Williams Trio take this beautiful carol to a late-night piano bar, with wonderful results.

- Sufjan Stevens makes a laid-back indie ballad out of Germany's beautiful Christmas hymn 'Lo How a Rose E'er Blooming'.

- Bert Jansch retains all the simplicity of 'In the Bleak Midwinter', adding his own folky spontaneity to create a gorgeous pop song.

- 'Little Drummer Boy' gets some unexpected urban edge from Lauryn Hill.

DID YOU KNOW?

In 1965 'Jingle Bells' was the first song ever broadcast from earth to space, when astronauts Tom Stafford and Wally Schirra from *Gemini 6A* decided to play a Christmas joke on Mission Control. Reporting to Control that they were seeing a suspicious unidentified object flying in a polar orbit, the astronauts then broke into a rendition of 'Jingle Bells' on a harmonica and sleigh bells that they had smuggled on to the spacecraft.

One of the earliest and most enduring of these popular carols is 'Jingle Bells'. Composed in 1857 (the same year, incidentally, as 'We Three Kings'), 'Jingle Bells' is one of the very first secular Christmas carols – at least, the first of a new generation. Its festive mood – more party song than religious hymn – and foot-stamping energy brings to mind the riotous numbers sung by the wassailers, and pieces like 'The Boar's Head Carol' – secular feast songs for public occasions that were set aside when Christmas took up residence in the church.

Although 'Jingle Bells' has evolved into a children's favourite, wholesome and unquestionably PG, its jolly story of a snowy sleigh ride may conceal an altogether less innocent story.

Jingle Bells

We know that the carol was composed by one James Lord Pierpont, an American organist and musician, but the question of where is more fraught. The towns of Medford, Massachusetts and Savannah, Georgia each lay claim to its composition with some fine civic plaques, but perhaps the carol itself gives the greatest clue as to the truth of the matter; snowy Christmases seem a far more natural part of a Massachusetts December than the rather warmer Savannah, as does sleigh-riding. Nineteenth-century Medford was home to a regular series of sleigh races, terrifying inhabitants as the rowdy competitors dashed up and down Salem Street. Another clue supporting Medford's claim lies in the carol's middle verse, rarely sung today.

> *A day or two ago*
> *I thought I'd take a ride*
> *And soon, Miss Fanny Bright*
> *Was seated by my side,*

The horse was lean and lank
Misfortune seemed his lot
He got into a drifted bank
And then we got upsot.

The final line is an interesting one. What is it that upsets the riders from their sleigh? Could it possibly be drunkenness (the chief industry of Medford at this time was distilling rum)? A 'sot' was slang for a drunk at the time, so it's possible that this little play on words is sneakily telling us what's really going on here. But whether this is the truth, or Savannah's rather tamer story of a song composed for a Sunday school Thanksgiving service, it's a history that's been all but lost from the song we know today.

Another song whose true history has been lost under ever-thicker layers of festive frosting and baubles is 'Rudolph the Red-Nosed Reindeer'. It's a Christmas carol that should by rights be the professional anthem of copywriters everywhere – the ultimate marketing jingle-turned-tradition. Rudolph was the creation of one Robert L. May, a staffer at the Montgomery Ward department stores. Tasked with creating a character to help sell a series of Christmas-themed colouring books in 1939, May created Rudolph, the plucky little reindeer whose unusual nose saves Christmas. A decade later, the store gave the copyright to May, whose storybook of Rudolph's adventures became a bestseller, inspiring his brother-in-law Johnny Marks to write his catchy song. One

> ### DID YOU KNOW?
>
> Rudolph the Red-Nosed Reindeer was very nearly christened Rollo or Reginald. Luckily for songwriter Johnny Marks (who would have had rather more difficulty making 'Reginald' scan), Robert L. May eventually settled on Rudolph instead.

big-name singer later (country-and-western artist Gene Autry), and the song too became a hit.

A Celluloid Christmas

It's thanks to cinema that we have many of our favourite Christmas songs, a number of them dating from the 1940s – the era of the musical comedy and singing stars Frank Sinatra, Judy Garland, Bing Crosby and Fred Astaire. If there's one song that sums up twentieth-century Christmas, a carol laced with just the right amount of nostalgic melancholy for the years gone by, it's 'White Christmas'. The song first appeared not, as many now believe, in the 1954 film *White Christmas*, but over a decade earlier in *Holiday Inn* – composed especially for the soundtrack by Irving Berlin. Although the song won an Academy Award for Best Original Song in 1942 and proved an instant hit with the public (who kept Bing Crosby's recording at the top of the Billboard Chart for 11 weeks in 1942, and ultimately made it the biggest-selling single of all time), it took Crosby himself a little longer to realise its magic. His response on first hearing the song? The deliciously understated, 'I don't think we have any problems with that one, Irving'.

The song may belong to a shiny celluloid age, geared to a very different market to its Victorian forebears, but part of the success of 'White Christmas' is that it taps into precisely the same kind of imagined nostalgia for a lost past. The carol was a favourite on the Armed Forces Network, requested by service personnel who recognised its yearning for familiar comforts, for Christmases 'just like the ones I used to know'. This streak of melancholy, a wistful sense of things lost as well as gained, is a surprisingly regular feature in Christmas songs, whether it's 'I'll be Home for Christmas', 'Blue Christmas' or even 'Last Christmas'. But nowhere is this smiling-through-tears fragility more poignantly captured than in 'Have Yourself a Merry Little Christmas'.

One of the big hits of Judy Garland's 1944 film *Meet Me in St. Louis*, the song very nearly didn't make it on to the soundtrack at all after a series of conflicts and false starts. First there was the difficulty with the melody itself. Songwriter Hugh Martin had been messing around with the 'madrigal-like' tune for a few days but, finding no way to resolve it, threw it away. Fortunately his writing partner Ralph Blane had overheard his attempts and together they dug through the wastepaper basket to rescue and complete it. Then there was the issue of the words. The song was intended for a scene towards the end of the film, the moment when Garland's character Esther finds herself in despair; forced to leave her beloved home and city, she sings a song to her little sister Tootie (Margaret O'Brien). Martin's initial lyric was, in his own words, 'lugubrious'.

Neither the director Vincente Minnelli nor Garland herself felt comfortable with such downbeat words, requesting that Martin replace them with something a little cheerier. As Garland put it: 'If I sing that to that sweet little Margaret O'Brien, they'll think I'm a monster!' After initially refusing, Martin eventually capitulated, rewriting the verse in the version we recognise today.

Christmas Goes Pop

But fashions change, and a public once happy to subsist on a festive diet of nostalgic melancholy and sweet-toothed delight now demands something just a little stronger to wash it all down. It says a lot that topping every recent survey and outperforming every rival when it comes to the best-loved contemporary Christmas songs is a blackly comic ballad of a failing relationship that was almost released with the title 'Christmas Eve in the Drunk Tank'.

That song is, of course, The Pogues and Kirsty MacColl's gloriously dark 'Fairytale of New York' (1988) – the ultimate anti-carol that medicates generations of mistletoe-and-starlight fantasies with its own beaten-up brand of festive cheer. Described by Pogues frontman Shane MacGowan in a 2012 interview with the *Guardian* as 'By far the most complicated song that I have ever been involved in writing and performing', 'Fairytale' took an astonishing two years to reach its final, freewheeling form, moving through many different incarnations and artists in the process.

As with all good carols its genesis is disputed, but one version has the band's producer, Elvis Costello, betting MacGowan and banjo player Jem Finer that they couldn't write a hit Christmas song that wasn't sentimental. The result is a curiously timeless fable. A man, down on his luck, is locked up in a drunk tank on Christmas Eve, when he hears an old man singing a folk song, which carries him back to a romance of his youth. Unusually, the woman in question also gets a say (though whether only in his dream is unclear), chiming in her account of events and later, when the story shifts to the present day, matching him insult for insult in a verse so colourfully abusive that as recently as 2007 BBC Radio 1 were censoring it during broadcast.

But for all its surface shock value and rejection of romance, 'Fairytale of New York' is a surprisingly traditional carol. Just look at the musical elements, a ballad with a big melody whose chorus breaks into a lilting Irish jig: dance and song. Somehow, in rejecting all the conventions of contemporary carols, The Pogues and MacColl took us right back to where it all started, to a rowdy singalong celebration of rhythm and melody.

We've come a long way from the silence and solemnity of King's Chapel, from the lone boy chorister, and even further from the Franciscans, and the shepherds listening to that first carol sung by the angels over Bethlehem. But if we're not to risk repeating the mistakes of the Victorians, who bowdlerised Christmas into precious piety by washing all the mud from folk carols and pagan customs, dressing them up in clean red robes and leading them to church, then we have to allow Christmas songs their place in the history of the carol. Their guitars, synthesisers, children's characters and novelty jumpers are never going to make it into King's Chapel, but then neither did the wassail songs that are their ancestors, the popular ballads and pub songs that are as authentic a part of this mongrel festival as any medieval carol.

END NOTES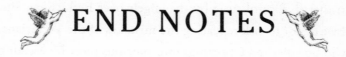

SOURCES

Chapter 4 A King's College Christmas

1. King's College Cambridge Archive Centre: KCA, MRJ/D/Milner-White.

2. King's College Cambridge Archive Centre: KCA, MRJ-C-4.

3. W.J. Margetson, *G.H.S. Walpole: A Memoir* (London: W. Gardner, Darton, 1930), p.8.

4. Arthur Christopher Benson, *The Life of Edward White Benson*, Vol. 1 (London: Macmillan, 1899), p. 76.

5. King's Cambridge Archive Centre: CSV/119.

6. King's Cambridge Archive Centre: CSV/119.

7. M.R. James, *Eton and King's* (London: Williams & Norgate, 1926), quoted in 1975 Nine Lessons and Carols Order of Service.

8. King's Cambridge Archive Centre: CSV/142.

9. Patrick Magee, *Highlands and Lowlands*, unpublished memoir, written permission given by executor, p. 11.

10. BBC Press Service, press release, 18 November 1958, p. 1.

11. *The Times* (27 December 1938).

12. King's College Cambridge Archive Centre: CVS/142.

13. Nicholas Nash, 'A History of A Festival of Nine Lessons and Carols', in Jean Michel Massing and Nicolette Zeeman, eds, *King's College Chapel 1515–2015* (London: Harvey Miller Publishers, 2014), p. 343.

14. Trevor Beeson, *In Tuneful Accord: The Church Musicians* (London, SCM Press, 2009), p. 139.

15. Quotes taken from sleeve notes, copyright Andrew Burn 2006, of *Christmas at St John's* (Hyperion Records). Full details of disc here: http://www.hyperion-records.co.uk/dc.asp?dc=D_CDA67576, accessed January 2016.

Chapter 5 Christmas Carols Today

1. William Owen, ed., *A Life In Music: Conversations with Sir David Willcocks and Friends* (Oxford, Oxford University Press, 2008), pp. 4–142.

2. BBC Written Archives', Caversham Park File T14/621.

3. BBC Written Archives', Caversham Park File T14/621.

4. Stuart Jeffries, 'King's College choir: meet the choirmaster', *Guardian* (2012, http://www.theguardian.com/music/2012/dec/19/kings-college-choir-choirmaster, accessed January 2016.

5. Midge Ure, *If I Was ... : An Enhanced Updated Autobiography*, (London: Acorn Digital Press), p.108, accessed February 2016.

MUSICAL EXTRACTS

The author and publishers have made all reasonable efforts to contact the copyright holders for permission, and apologise for any omissions or errors in the form of credit given. They would like to thank the following:

ACKNOWLEDGEMENTS

Without Carey Smith this book wouldn't have been started and without Grace Paul it would never have been finished, so a huge thank you goes to them and all their team at Penguin Random House. I'm also very grateful for the help of Dr Patricia McGuire, archivist at King's Cambridge, Sue Dickson at the BBC, James Whitbourn and the staff of the BBC Written Archive at Caversham Park. This book would have been infinitely poorer without the generosity of so many ex-King's musicians who shared their memories and thoughts with me. Chief among these is the astonishing David Briggs, whose memories are so important a part of this book, but also John Rutter, Bob Chilcott, Richard Suart, Richard Causton and Gabriel May. Without Stephen Drew and his kind interventions I wouldn't have had the opportunity to speak to so many of these fascinating people – thank you. Thanks also to Catherine Passingham for allowing me to quote portions of Patrick Magee's wonderfully vivid memoir. Lastly, all thanks to Ed Wilson for waiting so patiently, and of course to Peter Brooke for pretty much everything.

INDEX